1

GW00786439

To
Eric
with

AS FAR AS I CAN REMEMBER

This book is dedicated to all those ships that have passed in the night and to those who have stayed with me for the voyage.

AS FAR AS I CAN REMEMBER'

A BOUQUET GARNI OF CANDID MEMOIRS, 'OFF THE WALL' SHORT STORIES, QUIRKY VERSE AND, FOR GOOD MEASURE,

TWO ENDINGS!

By

TERRY JOHN WARD

Author of

'The Levelling Dust'

'The Artful Dodger and the Hero of the Forlorn Hope'

Co-editor of

'Are You the Man?'

Memories of life in the Trucial Oman Scouts

'TELL THE TRUTH AND SHAME THE DEVIL'

Acknowledgments

Grateful thanks to my son, Gary, for his patience and the outstanding technical assistance he has provided during the creation of this book and to Captain John Hopkins RA {Ret'd} for his kind help and valuable advice.

CONTENTS

LOST WORLDS {1}

LOST WORLDS {2}

A NOTE FROM THE AUTHOR

Sitting comfortably up here on my high horse, I make the observation that it is relatively easy for publishers to publish, critics to criticise and readers to read, then discard the efforts of writers; but please spare a kind thought for married male scribblers; they battle with might and main to find the opportunity to string a few sentences together in between their onerous domestic duties.

GK Chesterton once observed that the married writer frequently trips over the pram while on the way to his typewriter. That's only the half of it. Coleridge's thought processes were supposedly stopped dead in their tracks by a visit from a 'Person from Porlock', reducing Xanadu from an epic poem to a few lines. If he'd suffered from the amount of interruptions the modern married male does while writing, The Rime of the Ancient Mariner might be a whole lot shorter, too! Come to think of it, in that instance, it would have been a bit of a blessing!

Now, don't tell the missis about this, and with a nod in the direction of Messrs Gilbert & Sullivan, here's what I mean.

'Oh, the married writer's lot
A happy one is not,
For we suffer interruptions by the score.
When the Dyson starts a-screaming
It's a waste of time appealing,
'Coo, 'It's YOU who put the dirt upon the floor!'

Oh, the married writer's lot, a happy one is not
(I hope you know I'm talking modern men)
What with the shopping and the cooking,
Writing doesn't get a look in,
Domestic duties being mightier than the pen!
With our creative juices running

We begin to think there's fun in
What we are trying so hard to attain
But we lose the blasted flow
When she bellows orders from below;
And there we are with writers' block again!

Don't jump to conclusions. Wifely love is more important to me than literature; so is laughter. I am quietly confident that you will encounter all three within the pages of this book. In fact, all human life, or most of it, is here!

If I have omitted anything, it is merely due to the fact that I have no wish to hurt anyone's feelings.

Terry John Ward

Lost Worlds (1)

1

'There's always a better place to be,
Across the meadow and over the lea.'

Born in to one disappeared world, I was fortunate enough to
live for a while in a second.

First memories are something akin to watching brief snatches
of silent film featuring oneself.

Flash!

I am seated in a pushchair. My mother is hurrying it along a
country lane as an aerial dog-fight takes place above our heads.
My baby eyes gaze up at vapour trails creating pretty patterns
across the sky. There are no sounds in that memory-just images
and my imagined voice, squealing,

'Look, mummy, airplanes!'

Flash!

I am tottering about among rows of frosted Brussels sprouts
stalks, picking up pieces of shrapnel and placing them in a bag,
as a mobile gun, its long barrel pointing skywards like an
admonishing finger, is driven noisily past our garden gate.

Flash!

A sock hangs at the foot of an iron bedstead standing beneath a
sloping, attic roof. Awestruck by the magic and mystery of
Christmas, I scramble for my presents; an apple, an orange, the

traditional lump of coal, a comic book and a wooden toy. Treasures!

Flash again.

I now see my small self shivering wiith a strange excitement beside a railway line. I place a row of pebbles on a humming rail, before cowering in a ditch beside the permanent way. The train goes hurtling past, crunching the stones to dust and enveloping me in smoke and steam.

Was I indulging in some form of innate wickedness? I simply don't know.

Ah, this is better! From the age of six, or thereabouts, I have almost continuous memories. I can now fast forward or reverse wind them at will.

Cynical attitudes and Monty Python's 'Born in a Cardboard Box' sketch have made it impossible to write seriously about poverty-stricken childhoods, so I will simply say that, together with my four brothers, I was starved of everything except parental care, food- and freedom. By the latter, I mean that we always had hundreds of acres of Kent or Sussex woods and fields to roam about in; streams to swim in and redundant Second World War gun emplacements to make camps in. We often defended these areas from hordes of German invaders, engaging in bloody hand-to-hand fighting with an imaginary foe. If it wasn't Germans it was Sioux Indians on the warpath.

My brothers and I only lacked clothing we were not ashamed to wear to school, and such everyday comforts as carpets on the floor and sheets and pillowcases on our beds. I first enjoyed the luxury of those particular items when I went in to hospital at the age of twelve.

It was much worse for our barrel-chested, bull-headed father and surprisingly gentile, quietly spoken mother, because they had to do everything they could to 'keep body and soul together'. A seemingly ill-matched pair, they both worked on the land. Father never took a holiday, apart from having a day out at the seaside with his family from time to time. My mother kept house and undertook seasonal farm work. Dependent on where we happened to be living at the time, this could be anything from picking hops to stacking corn stooks or gathering up root crops, after they had been spun out of the ground by a horse-drawn potato-plough.

Skilled in all the crafts that made a good farm labourer, my father's only freedom in life was the freedom to move on. Obtaining a new job was never a problem for him. He would thumb through the 'Situations Vacant' pages in the Farmers' Weekly, get on his bone-shaker bike and set off for some distant farm, returning, many hours later to declare that he'd secured a new job. The farm owner was a good man. The house we were going to live in had everything we wanted and the village was 'just down the road'; all of which seldom proved to be true. My father obtained new employment very easily because he had great, gruff charm and although he wouldn't have had a hope in hell of passing a written examination on agriculture, he understood everything about it. Years of experience had made him an expert on animal husbandry. He could also 'lay' a hedge, reap, sow, stack, thatch, and hand milk twenty or more cows twice a day, seven days a week. He could plough a straight furrow and handle a wagon and four horses. He could manage hop gardens and orchards and understood the complex workings of threshing machines, the steam engines that powered them, and much more besides. His reward for all this was pittance wages and a roof over his family's head.

During the war, while living close to a fighter station in what became known as 'Doodle-Bug Alley' he even managed to obtain work in Shropshire for the duration, rather than allow the authorities to evacuate his children to a safer area. No-one was going to split his family up!

Sometimes it was indeed 'Cold Comfort Farm'

Moving on, a set of fire tongs that didn't belong to us were thrown on to the cattle truck that had been sent to collect us. Well, they'd hosed it down beforehand, hadn't they? The vindictive farm owner, who also 'owned' the fire tongs we'd accidentally taken with us, had my father arrested. He was charged with theft, found guilty and fined ten shillings in a magistrate's court.

The dilapidated farm cottages we lived in were, more often than

not, lit by oil lamps. The waste convenience would be 'out the back' and a well in the garden provided us with water. House bricks, heated in the oven and wrapped in scarves, warmed our beds in winter.

I progressed from babyhood to childhood, oblivious of the war, food rationing and practically everything else in the larger world. Wherever we happened to be living, my brothers and I remained isolated from the rest of society. Sadly, we never stayed anywhere long enough to form friendships at school or with the children of other farm labourers.

Those small farms were invariably a good three miles from villages whose names read like chapter headings taken from Cobbett's Rural Rides: Hale Street, Eastling, Rotherfield, Jarvis Brook, Hartfield, Wadhurst, Wickhambreaux, Chevening, Mayfield, Ham Street, White Hill, Cowden, Scaynes Hill, Beckley....

In the main, these were small communities living in peace and quiet. The nearest one got to a 'Take-Away' was the weekly visit of a mobile fish and chip shop and the only commuters were ducks making their way to the village pond. The church, village hall, pub, blacksmith, garage and a grocers' shop cum post office, where one could buy anything from a coal scuttle to a pound of freshly-sliced bacon, satisfied everyone's immediate needs.

There wasn't much money about, except for those who lived in grand places with names such as The Grange, Glebe House or The Manor. Spray-can graffiti hadn't arrived from New York and the only criminals around, were poachers (including my father) and those using the red petrol reserved for agricultural purposes in their bull-nosed Morris or Austin 7. The only 'kids' to be found were baby goats. In the working-class world, boys aged fifteen or under, were children. At sixteen they were young men. Those teen age 'Gap Years' that emerged for young people sometime during the mid-1950's, delayed their maturing process somewhat, especially after National Service ceased.

How close to nature we country-bred urchins were in those early, post-war days! We became familiar with the creatures around us; wild as well as domestic. Morose cattle, docile sheep and noble horses were nothing to worry about, but stinking ferrets would give you a nasty bite when you were feeding them mice. Bulls and Billy goats were to be avoided at all costs! Flittering bats were frightening because rumour had it they would nest in your hair if you weren't careful. Those flittering creatures were just as dangerous as eating the ends of bananas, which as everyone knew, were deadly poisonous!

Badgers' and slinking foxes, crows as black as night and doves as white as snow, all lived together, although not necessarily in harmony, in a world that the internal combustion engine had scarcely penetrated. Those noisy intrusions had a curiosity value and captured my interest. When the butcher's or baker's van stopped at our house, I would give them a close examination; running my grubby fingers over their warm bonnets, testing their door handles and making engine noises as I grasped an imaginary steering wheel. The delivery man would return; ruffling my hair before climbing in to his vehicle. The baker would sometimes give me a couple of sticky buns to share with my brothers; but we never got a sausage from the butcher!

A journey by 'bus was a rare treat, although the first one I made, with brothers, Mick and Owen, in charge of me, turned in to a near-death experience.

'Tup's never been the same since he fell off the 'bus!' became a family saying.

I didn't fall off- I jumped!

They took me to Tonbridge to see Walt Disney's cartoon version of Pinocchio; my first 'bus ride, first cinema visit, and first brush with death.

Returning home, with the three of us sitting together on a long, back seat., I began to recognise the landscape we were passing through.

I knew that barn, that oast house, those trees… Panic set in as the 'bus neared the point where I knew we had to get off. IT WASN'T GOING TO STOP! Before anyone, including the conductor, could prevent me from doing so, I stood up, took a couple of tiny steps to the platform at the open doorway, and knowing absolutely nothing about the laws of physics, I jumped.

They say my unconscious form was taken to a doctor's surgery in the back of a butcher's van that happened to be passing.

When I returned to the land of the living, the first thing I noticed was that a good deal of my small body had been painted a nice shade of violet with what proved to be iodine.

Sometime after this close call, I remember my mother bursting in to tears when it was announced on the radio that Tommy Handley, of ITMA fame, had died.

ITMA (It's That Man Again) had more catch phrases than any other radio show, before or since.

'Can I do you now, sir?'

'I don't mind if I do!'

'Don't forget the diver!'

'I go- I come back'.

'After you, Claude. No, after you, Cecil.'

BBC radio had played a remarkable role in sustaining and informing millions of people, including my parents, throughout the Second World War. Apart from accurately reporting the allies' defeats and victories, it entertained the Home Front with unequalled comedy shows such as, Variety Bandbox and Much Binding in the Marsh.

As a family, we huddled round our one luxury, a battery and accumulator powered Cossor radio. It was a treasure trove of fun, entertainment and information. It could be scary, as well, if one listened to Valentine Dyall's voice in 'The Man in Black'.

The next occasion I saw mother cry was when King George V1 died in 1952. Many people must have been in tears that day. Both of the schoolteachers at Hartfield Primary School certainly were. Forbidding the two classes to make any noise whatsoever, they led us out to the playground and made us stand in silent rows while the Union Jack that was raised to the top of the flagpole before assembly every morning, was lowered to half-mast.

I became familiar with the taste and texture of every thing remotely edible that grew, wild or cultivated. I followed rabbit tracks to the edge of darkly sinister woodland; removing their dead or dying carcasses from snares set by my father. I was skinning those creatures at a very early age, and wringing the necks of chickens as well. Death was all around. Shot pigeons fluttering to earth, the pathetic corpses of fledglings, fallen from nests in spring, drowned sheep after a winter flood, rats smoked out of their maze of tunnels to be shot or clubbed as they emerged. I watched barn owls swooping on mice scurrying around hay stacks, and saw the devastation left behind by a fox after it had dug its way in to a chicken run.

Life was rampant too; lambs, calves, kids, chicks and foals were born. Hares engaged in boxing matches, skylarks chirped their ecstatic songs as they rose higher and higher in to an early summer sky, and skeins of geese made orderly, elegant flights across the Romney Marshes.

Ah, the marshes! Aged about seven, and living on the edge of them, I fell in love with the wonderfully named, Primrose Smart, while attending Ham Street Primary School. It was a brief romance because my father soon took us off to- I can't remember where- but:

'I once held hands with Primrose Smart
As we danced around the May-Pole tree.
I could feel the beating of my heart
When she turned her head and smiled at me.
I once held hands with Primrose Smart
As we dangled our bare feet in a stream
And watched the shoals of sticklebacks dart
Among the water plants, softly green.'

Two dramatic events occurred while I lived near Ham Street. The first of these was on Guy Fawkes Night. The owner, Mr. Godden, allowed us farm boys to build a bonfire in his farmyard and generously provided us with a large number of fireworks. Came the night, and we were ready to bake potatoes and chestnuts in the embers of the fire. A bushel basket, full of fireworks, was left in what seemed to be a safe place. It wasn't. The very first rocket to be lit by one of the farm labourers contrived to rise a few feet into the air, twist, turn and fall straight into the basket. A spectacular but short-lived sound and light show followed. Soaring rockets and a series of loud, staccato explosions! They certainly kept our heads down!

The second, more serious, drama occurred on Christmas Eve that same year. My brothers and I were gathered round the kitchen table with our parents, belatedly making paper chains; using a flour and water paste to stick them together. We were as poverty stricken as Bob Cratchit's family but happy in our ignorance of how other people lived.

There was a loud hammering on the door on what really was,

'A dark and stormy night'.

Wind and rain made their presence felt when my father opened the door to find a member of the Godden family standing there, water dripping from his Sou-Wester. His brother had gone off into the night in a worrying state of mind and he wanted father to help search for him.

He returned home in the early hours of Christmas morning, soaked through to the skin, to find us still wide-awake in the kitchen. Stories of ghosts, goblins and headless horsemen fevered our imaginations. Our feelings were prescient because the search party had discovered the missing man's dead body in some remote sheds, known to us all as Black Lodges. He had committed suicide.

My father's normally booming voice was, for once, rather quiet as he ordered us boys to get to bed.

Winding the memory machine back a little; the winter of 1947, one of the worst suffered in twentieth century England, also had a dramatic moment for me.

We were living in a wooden bungalow beside a country lane that roamed through the hills above the village of Jarvis Brook, in East Sussex.

January was mild until the third week, but after that, Southern England found itself in the grip of snow and ice, with record breaking low temperatures. It snowed continuously throughout the whole of February.

Before the outlying areas became completely snowed in, a council funded taxi continued to pick us farm children up and deliver us to the village primary school.

Once there, we would sit in our classrooms, wearing our coats and scarves throughout the day; breaking the ice in the bottles of milk we were issued with before swallowing it. A drink so cold it gave us brief headaches.

One morning, the taxi driver lost control of his Austin 14, with its wood and leather interior, while negotiating a steep, ice covered hill. Despite everything he could do to stop it, the car slid across the road junction at the bottom the hill, went straight through a hedge and plunged in to a deep snow drift in the field beyond. No seat belts, of course, but no-one was hurt.

The driver extricated us from the car and walked us the rest of the way to the school. Nobody cried

My brother, Brian, was born in a chilly room in that bungalow. Once again, we were snowed in, so a police vehicle had to bring the mid-wife through the blocked country lanes, to mother. In arctic conditions, they battled and battered their way to our front door; arriving in time for the mid-wife to do her work. Robin had been born, uneventfully, in 1943, so now we were brothers five.

Sometimes, the strain on our family purse was simply too great. At Cowden, the Reverend Hart-Dyke was kind enough to buy me an essential pair of boots so that I could continue to go to school. I was a choir boy and one of a team of bell-ringers in the parish church, until moving on, of course.

Belief in God came naturally to me then. My faith was strengthened by the beauty of the churches, the traditional hymns we sang and by reading the King James bible. Villagers attended the same form of Sunday service as they had since the reformation. The Church of England hadn't become a weather vane, pointing in whatever direction the wind blew it. I thought such tranquil continuity could never be changed or broken. I was mistaken.

2

Body and Soul Food

I don't think it is putting it too strongly when I write that I was of the earth and lived off its bounty. Cob nuts, blackberries, the sweet stalks of certain grasses, crab apples and what rustic children referred to as 'bread n' cheese'- spring's first growth on hawthorn hedges. I worked too; docking thistles in cow-pastures for half a crown a day, sawing logs, chopping kindling, or weeding dad's vegetable garden; taking the opportunity to pull a fresh carrot from the ground as I did so. Knocking most of the dirt from it, I would crunch away, quite contentedly. The finest protection from developing allergies is to stay close to nature from birth. I certainly did that!

From time to time, I would be detailed to bring the cows in for the evening milking. Myrtle, Buttercup, Daisy et al, would all 'fall-in' the moment I entered the field; passing through the five-barred gate leading to the farmyard, in single file. Without any encouragement from me, they would amble nonchalantly into the cowshed and enter their own particular stall. They knew the drill.

I was perfectly at ease among cows, docile sheep, snorting, rough skinned pigs and amusingly scatty ducks and hens; but belligerent geese tended to treat small boys with contempt, while bantams did what came naturally to them if you were late shutting them up for the night. They roosted in trees-and were the very devil to get down again.

The Ward boys all tracked a good deal of what mother referred to as, 'clean dirt', in to our house. We were, in fact, a modern-day health and safety officer's worst nightmare. Dangerous, unsupervised play was the order of the day. At weekends and after school, we went out and about, armed to the teeth with catapults, wooden rifles, bows and arrows - and knives to make them with. Whips and spinning tops were popular toys for children in the late 1940's. Colourful wooden cones spun and propelled along footpaths, or in playgrounds, by cracking whips. We slid down haystacks, used clods of earth as hand grenades and rode rickety, homemade boxcarts down the steepest hills we could find; either deliberately crashing them at the bottom or bringing them to a halt by using our booted feet as brakes. In the twenty first century, officialdom would faint away at the very sight of it all.

Deprivation, one of the excuses used to explain away delinquency, and worse, somehow failed to turn us into a criminal gang. Instinctively, we followed the unwritten laws of the countryside; closing farm gates behind us to prevent stock from straying, skirting fields where crops were growing and looking after the camp fires we built. We had a set of rules to follow at home, and it was the natural right of any adult to discipline a child if he or she got out of line.

My parents had oft-repeated sayings and expressions that have become lodged forever in my mind.
Mother would look out of the kitchen window, watching storm clouds gathering in the distance.
'It looks like it's raining over Will's Mother's.'

I never discovered who the mysterious Will was.

She would take one look at us when we came in from the garden, and say, 'You boys look as though you've been pulled through a hedge, back'ards.'

Father's expressions were a little more acerbic and were usually spouted after he had picked up the Daily Mirror at breakfast time. He would look at a headline featuring a 'High-Nob', and say,

'The trouble with the likes o' them is they think their shit don't stink.'

Or, after reading the details concerning the government's budget, or about a new law that had been passed,

'We'd all be better off livin' in the middle of a bloody great wood.'

He was quite right, of course. Independent, self sufficient people such as we were, didn't require any governing. We could manage very well without it, thank you.

'I don't want any bugger telling me what to do. I can take care of meself.'

If Mick and I returned from a bike ride and began bragging about how we'd pedalled all the way to the top of a steep hill, dad would be inclined to bring us down a peg or two.

'You just be glad it weren't Bluebell 'ill'. That's a real 'ill, that is. You wouldn't get up that one in a 'urry, I can tell you.'

This hill of myth and legend is near Maidstone, but never having seen it we could only imagine its Himalayan height.

We know that its gradient was too much of a challenge for horse drawn omnibuses providing a service between Maidstone and Chatham. An 'Upper Bell' and a 'Lower Bell' were tolled to give notice to passengers that it was time to begin either walking up or down the hill to make their connection.

If you ever find yourself driving your car up Bluebell Hill at midnight, don't be too surprised if you find that you have a travelling companion in the form of a ghost sitting in the passenger seat. She is, purportedly, the harmless spirit of a girl killed in a road accident on the night before her wedding.

Not keen on ghosts? All right, try running a certain number of times around the dolmen known as Kits Coty. Don't ask me how many, the amount keeps changing! Get it right and your dreams will come true.

The old Pilgrims' Way passes hard by Bluebell Hill. If one sits quietly by the side of it on a day in summer; just as the heroine does in Powell and Pressburger's surreal 1944 film, 'A Canterbury Tale', one can easily conjure up the sound of a troubadour playing a lute as he entertains a jolly group of 13th century travellers during their journey to Canterbury Cathedral.

Bluebell Hill

The name speaks of gentle pleasures,
Picnics, the gathering of wild flowers
And secret trysts where lovers meet at leisure.
But see the hill's calciferous jowl
Below its furrowed brow?
That once gave sanctuary from Sabre-Tooths
Prowling the plain below.
Those slopes lush grass;
Fed by battle blood in Hengist's reign,
Bore the tread of travellers
To a martyred bishop's tomb.
Then, during those heroic dogfight days
When England stood alone,
 Suffered from the impact
Of a pilot's shattered 'plane.
Now, ascending and descending
Juggernauts drown out the clash of
Ancient armies, pious pilgrims

And the primaeval one,
Whose span of life was measured
By the rising, setting sun.

  In the late 1940's, artificial lights were still few and far between in remote corners of Kent and Sussex, so when the moon was down, the nights were truly dark. They were silent too; apart from vague rustlings emanating from woods and hedgerows and the occasional screeching bark of a fox.

  At the end of a track which sloped away from a narrow country lane, three miles from the village of Beckley, we quickly settled in to a ramshackle cottage - we had become experts at doing that- and went to our beds.

  Mick raised the alarm in the middle of the night. Someone, or something, was trying to break in through his bedroom window! We all dashed downstairs, grabbed what weapons we could lay our hands on: a handbill, a broom, a poker- and rushed outside, only to find that the 'intruder' was nothing more than the overhanging branch of a tree, tapping gently against the bedroom window in a stiff breeze. I don't know about the others, but the incident scared the pants off me- except that I wasn't wearing any.

  The Ward brothers only ventured forth from their land-locked islands to attend school or go to the village garage with a radio accumulator that required re-charging. Two hundred acre islands, one hundred and sixty acres; it all depended upon father's latest job. However long or short our stay, we always turned the farms into adventure playground. Woods, hop gardens, orchards, streams, corn fields and pastures, became jungles, great rivers, forests and prairies.

  Those of us who went to school could graze our way to and from them throughout the seasons. There was always something tasty to be had, either in the hedgerows or just beyond. Apples and cherries on low hanging boughs, cob nuts, crab apples, blackberries, succulent grasses, ears of corn. I particularly enjoyed eating cattle-cake, myself. Filched from an open sack in the cowshed, these oxo cube sized, compressed nutrients were very tasty as far as I was concerned. I was still light years away from enjoying chef's perks. Moules marinierre, tarte tatin and Roquefort cheese had yet to replace mousetrap cheddar, a crust of bread smeared with margarine and dipped in sugar, or a bowl of thick, grey porridge covered in black treacle.

Forgive me if I dwell further on the subject. of food.

The first thing father did when we arrived at yet another crumbling cottage was to start sorting out the vegetable garden and setting up a chicken run. His night forays would bring in plenty of snared rabbits for mother to turn into those rich stews and crusty pies I mentioned. Sunday afternoon jaunts with a .410 shotgun under his arm would result in father chucking dead wood pigeons or the occasional hare, onto the kitchen table. I was right there, skinning, plucking and gutting; my child-fingers covered in sticky, black blood, fur, or feathers.

Removing the skin of a rabbit in one piece holds a strange fascination. After paunching Brer Rabbit and removing its innards, you begin by pushing the back legs out of their furry covering. This leaves you free to pull the skin and fur towards its head. The flesh is revealed. How remarkably smooth and clean it is! After pushing the front legs clear, a sharp tug and you will find yourself holding the complete skin in your bloody, little hands.

Rabbit Stew:

Joint one skinned, head chopped off, paunched and washed rabbit (Retain the liver). Season with the old s and p and place in a deep pan with two sliced onions, a few cloves and some shredded lemon peel. Simmer with the pan lid on for about thirty minutes. Remove the cloves with a slotted spoon and thicken the sauce with beurre manie (a flour and butter mix formed into pellets and mixed into the stock). Add balls of forcemeat* and simmer for a few more minutes; season to taste.

*To make forcemeat: finely chop the rabbits liver together with a thick slice of ham, 8oz of chicken breast, 4oz. suet, some breadcrumbs, mace, parsley and thyme. Mix together with an egg yolk. Form into balls and fry them before adding them to the stewed rabbit.

When I was eleven, or thereabouts, my father left me alone with a gigantic shire horse and a seed drill, to plant up the harrowed acres of a far-off field. Dad was experienced enough to know that the horse would know what to do; which is more than I did.

Up and down the field we went, the shire turning at each end without any prompting from me, and stopping obediently when I needed to refill the drill box. That horse had power and dignity in full measure. In co-operating with me, it seemed to be saying,

'Don't worry, boy. I can tell you're an amateur. I'll help you out this time.'

I judged my lunch break by the rumblings in my stomach and the position of the sun. My good companion kindly lowered its great head to my level so that I could place a feed bag over it. Grain for him and a doorstep cheese sandwich, washed down with cold tea, for me.

I had a feeling of oneness with everything around me; sensing that I was re-enacting a task that had been carried out by a boy wearing a smock at the time of the Tolpuddle Martyrs.

I wasn't wearing a smock, but my boots were just as scuffed and down at heel as his would have been!

One of my teachers arrived at my home one evening to speak to my parents. I was about to take the 11+ examination. Confident that I would pass with flying colours, she had secured a place for me on a Royal Navy Training Ship. It was mine if they would permit me to go. They wouldn't.

3

'Why, he is a common labouring boy!'

{Estella's remark about Pip in Great Expectations}

I passed the 11+ examination and was accepted by East Grinstead Grammar School. This encouraging event was about to put enormous and probably unmanageable financial strain on my parents, so perhaps what followed was fortuitous as far as they were concerned.

My left foot seemed determined to continue forming itself into a Roman arched bridge; toes and heel on the ground, and in between, room enough for a water boatman to pass through. Impossible to diagnose at the time, the deformity was an early symptom of a genetic disorder that hid itself away for many years then struck without further warning. As you will discover, the damn thing ruined my chances of having a grammar school education. It also had a devastating effect on my physical well being when I was much older.

An orthopaedic surgeon performed an operation during which he broke and re-set the bones in the troublesome foot; keeping everything in position by means of metal plates, top and bottom, secured by nuts and bolts.

Oh, the luxury of my hospital bed's crisp white sheets and pillowcases! I was soon in love with the immaculate, caring Ward Sister, as well.

My already romantic soul was deeply moved when, on Christmas Eve, a group of pretty nurses filed into the dimly lit children's' ward, carrying flickering candles. Gathering round the Christmas tree, they sang sweet, melodic carols to us. How blissful it was.

After convalescing at home for a few weeks and having those bolts withdrawn from my foot, I was eager to return to the classroom. All right, so I was a swot; want to make something of it? Before being permitted to do so, however, I was summoned to appear before an Educational Assessment Board in Tunbridge Wells. My poor parents, born in to a world of deference and forelock tugging, feared officialdom and avoided having anything to do with people in expensive suits. They would run a mile rather than face their kind; which is why, at the age of twelve, I found myself standing alone and unrepresented in front of three such types.

They seemed nonplussed when this appallingly scruffy and unhygienic looking boy whizzed through the exam papers they had set before him. I had a brain then. At school, I had a tendency to shoot a hand into the air, eager to answer a question before the teacher had even finished writing it on the blackboard.

Ragged and forlorn, like some latter day Oliver Twist, I stood facing my assessors across their imposing desk, making the silent plea.

'Please, sir, can I have some more education? I'm hungry for it.'

At the end of a hurried consultation, the leader of the trio decided my fate in one, never to be forgotten, sentence.

'I see his father's a farm labourer; better teach the boy a trade, eh?'

And that's how I found myself attending Bexhill Technical

School; yes, you've guessed it; dad had changed jobs yet again. We had moved from Hartfield and were now living at Hurst Green.

Being what one might call a 'budding academic' I was at odds with woodwork, plumbing, metalwork and bricklaying lessons, although as far as the last subject is concerned, I still know what a Flemish Bond is!

To give the school its due, it did introduce me to the likes of Peer Gynt, Prester John and Richard the Third; not forgetting my life-long friend, Barry Peter Dicks- I said I'd give him a mention.

My, never to be forgotten, friend and father-in-law, Charlie Underhill, once said to me:

'A boy alone? Ah, there's a boy for you! Put two boys together and you've only got half a boy. With three boys, you've got no boys at all.'

He was right, of course.

I travelled from Etchingham on a school train that delivered children to various senior schools in Bexhill.

Whoever decided that it would be perfectly safe to allow dozens of youngsters of both sexes, aged between eleven and sixteen, to do this without any form of supervision, must have been both incredibly stupid and stupendously naïve. Girls and weakling boys were thrown to the wolves that prowled those corridor-carriages. The events that took place were nothing short of scandalous and would have made the pages of the Sunday papers if reporters had got wind of it. Their being no-one to stop them, a gang of young, male predators went from compartment to compartment on a daily basis; even changing coaches at stations in order to interfere with as many of the schoolgirls as possible. Admittedly, some of their targets were just as interested in having close encounters as the boys were; offering themselves up to be endlessly groped and fondled. Others fought against being mauled about by boys off the leash, but they were usually overwhelmed by sheer numbers. I hope most sincerely that the abuse they suffered caused them no lasting psychological damage.

Years later, when I raised this subject with two 'old boys' from the technical school, they both recalled that while these rapacious antics were going on, I could be found, sitting in the corner of a compartment, writing short stories!.

Although most of the young passengers behaved very well, there was ruthless bullying, too. Boys who were slightly odd, weedy, or different in some way or other, were hassled, jeered at and physically assaulted. Flashman was alive and well and living in East Sussex. Early on, a small group known to one and all as the 'Robertsbridge Boys' attempted to make my life a misery, simply because I preferred sitting in a compartment, scribbling in exercise books, to joining their malicious ranks. I had heard they were out to 'get me', so when they barged in, I was ready for them. It was 'backs to the wall' stuff. After I'd lashed out several times with a tightly knotted scarf, causing one or two of them a little pain and suffering, they left me alone.

I am sorry to say that William Golding's depiction of how some totally unrestrained children would behave, as in Lord of the Flies, was far more accurate than RM Ballantyne's altruistic view of them in The Coral Island. My own eyes were opened to the truth of things. One might say that my days of innocence were nearly over. I was learning that life wasn't going to be all honey, out there in the big, wide world.

One morning, as the train was passing through Mountfield Tunnel, near Battle, one of the 'weedy' types, saddled with what was viewed to be the equally 'weedy' Christian name, Mervyn, was pursued into the compartment where I sat in my usual place. Crying hysterically, he opened the carriage door and attempted to leap out. I made a grab for him and managed to pull him on to a seat. While the poor wretch sat there snivelling, I slammed the wildly swinging door shut, squashing one of my thumbs in its jamb as I did so.

With the compartment half full of engine smoke, the bully boys, knowing that they'd had a narrow escape from being responsible for Mervyn's death; an event that, if it had happened, could not possibly be kept secret, called it a day.

There were no adult witnesses to the incident of course, and we certainly weren't going to tell anyone about it. The immutable law being, 'don't tell the grown-ups'; they lived in their world while we lived in ours. T'was ever thus.

I didn't feel heroic about the fact that I'd probably saved Mervyn's life; my squashed thumb hurt too much.

I have often wondered how that unfortunate boy got on in later life. I even developed a story about someone very much like him. My much abused character became very rich, sought out his tormentors and had his revenge. Unfortunately, someone else wrote a very similar book before I could write mine.

And what became of the bully boys? Did they end up in loveless marriages or in gaol, or did they get on in the world by being ruthless? I picture them spending their ill-gotten gains in night clubs; swaggering about dressed in expensive suits, with a tart on their arm and flash cars in their garages. See the child-see the man.

When I was fifteen, Mr. Barnes, my form master and English teacher at Bexhill Tech, introduced me to Mr. Parsons, the owner of a chain of Sussex newspapers. After looking at some of my written work, he offered to give me a job as a cub reporter when I reached my sixteenth birthday. Oh, joy!

4

The 50th Regiment of Foot
And the Retreat to Corunna

Losing myself many times in the works of Charles Dickens and C S Forester's novels set during the Napoleonic Wars, inspired me to write The Artful Dodger and the Hero of the Forlorn Hope, featuring the further adventures of CD's immortal character. One of the 'flashbacks' in the book relates the real-life experiences of the 50th Regiment of Foot, later, the Royal West Kent Regiment, during the retreat to Corunna; the Peninsular Wars equivalent to Dunkirk in the Second World War. An outgunned British Expeditionary Force miraculously escapes by sea to fight again. These events are viewed through the eyes of the man who was to become the Artful Dodger's mentor, Abel Garnett.

The Retreat to Corunna

North-east of Vimiero, on the lower slopes of the forested mountains, Privates Johnny Rose and Abel Garnett formed part of the two companies that had taken up their positions, led from the front by Captain Snow. Sounds of battle permeated every fibre of their being as the French advanced through the chestnut trees; a mass of blue and white uniforms, revealed and concealed by swirling smoke. Musket balls whizzed and flicked over the men of the 50th Foot, showering them with leaves and twigs as they returned fire under disciplined orders.

'We can't stand 'ere much longer!' Johnny yelled at Abel above the din. 'Why don't Captain Snow let us fall back?'

'Snow's dead, I think. I thought I saw him fall in that first volley. I can't see him waving his sword anymore. It must be Captain what's 'is name who's in charge now.'

Abel levelled his musket, along with over a hundred others, and pulled the trigger. The blast of fire seemed to send a shudder through the ranks as they became enveloped in choking fumes. 'Coote,' Abel said, grounding the butt of his musket to begin re-loading. 'Captain Coote; he's in command now.'

Another hail of French musket balls cut through and over them, creating the all too familiar screams of pain.

A hoarse voice began ordering,
'Fall back, men. Fall back!'

'Well, alleluia!' Johnny cheered. 'Come on, Abe; let's get out of here.'

Both companies retreated up the sloping ground in an untidy scramble as their ranks became broken up by the trees. The cheering voices of thousands of French soldiers scenting victory threatened to drown out the noise of the British cannon blasting away on top of the ridge.

'There's our lines!' The rest of the battalion was drawn up on the crest as well, fanning out on both sides of the batteries. Companies A and D were ordered to halt, one hundred yards from what they perceived to be safety.

The hoarse voice of Captain Coote brought them to a halt. 'We'll stand here, men. Face the enemy and fire on command.'

The stentorian roars of sergeants encouraged the men to form a single, ragged line. More orders compelled them to pour regular volleys into the approaching enemy. They could see their faces now, just as black with powder smoke as theirs were.

'Who gave that order to stand?' Johnny Rose shouted in Abel's ear. 'We could have bin up there with the battalion!'

Abel looked over his shoulder, seeking the British position. While Coote's two companies kept their attention, the battalion was beginning a maneuver that would allow them to outflank the French.

'Look, Johnny; the cavalry's going off to the left and the battalion's shifting to the right. They're trying to flank 'em, by thunder!'

Without thinking about it, Abel worked through the reloading and firing procedure; hearing, and not hearing the bellowed orders. He was a small part of a huge machine; a deafening, smoking, precision machine that would need to be destroyed completely before it would grind to a halt. Every twenty seconds, or so, it discharged fire, smoke and musket balls. Intricate patterns of movement following each volley, as the reloading procedures were carried out.

A commotion arose on their left. The sound of cheering British voices caused the machine to break up into individual human beings.

'We've outflanked the frogs - look at 'em run!'

In a second, they too were cheering madly.
'Let the buggers run,' Johnny said. 'I'm done in.'

He sat down suddenly on the ground as the order, 'Cease fire' was given.

All along the line, men were doing the same. The abrupt easing of the peril they had been in, leaving them desperately parched and weary.

Myriads of knapsacks bounced on the backs of French soldiery as they retreated through the trees below. The British were rolling up their left flank causing terrible carnage. Abel could detect the sounds of dragoons crashing through woods, somewhere out of sight. He sighed and wiped a grimy hand over his smoke-blackened face. Lord, he was thirsty!

After the heat of battle, came the anti-climax. The regiment languished for several weeks in an encampment near Lisbon. Fevers and outbreaks of dysentery swept through the ranks. Diseases caused as many deaths in the regiments as encounters with the enemy did. The wretched camp followers and their children suffered along with the rest of them.

Right on cue, just when the 50th began their march to Salamanca, the late October skies began discharging endless torrents of rain upon their columns.

They learnt again what it was like to go without food, march endless miles in worn out boots and cope with unrelenting downpours while negotiating difficult terrain.

There were few stoics among the regiment. Most of them cursed the country, the French, their officers and their sergeants, and when they could think of nothing else to curse, they turned on each other.

Kept ignorant of tactics and grand plans, the common soldiery only knew that, Wellesley being elsewhere, they were part of Sir John Moore's forces marching on a place called Salamanca; wherever that was. What was to happen after they got there, only God and the officers knew.

They were a month on the road, and the further they went, the worse things became for them. The villages grew meaner and their inhabitants ever more unwelcoming. Spending nights in stinking stables and pig sties became a luxury compared to sleeping in crudely constructed, temporary shelters.

A good part of their footslogging days were spent putting shoulders to ox carts, assisting them up mud- caked, precipitous tracks. On one occasion a span of bullocks, unable to sustain the upward impetus of a munitions wagon, gave up the unequal struggle. Abel barely had time to drag Johnny out of the way before it slid over the spot he'd been occupying and fell in to a ravine. The unfortunate animals gave out despairing bellows as they disappeared into the void.

In the Guadarrama mountains, temperatures fell low enough for men to freeze to death in their sleep. Some did.

Then the 50th's morale was boosted by the news that they would soon be descending into warmer climes.

It was several days before the last of them arrived at Salamanca; long after the main army had made their way through the narrow cobbled streets of the town.

In early December, with the regiments still recovering from their exertions, rumours began to pass among them again. A vastly superior French force, led by Marshal Soult, one of Napoleon's elite commanders, was fast approaching. The 50th were ordered to advance on Valladolid as a feint to draw his forces away from Madrid. They were on the march once more. This time they had heavy snow falls and the cold blast of winter winds to contend with.

On December 19th, after a forced march of eleven hours, the

column staggered, exhausted, into the town of Mayorga, where they were reunited with the balance of Moore's tattered army.

Thirty thousand officers and men found what comforts they could in and around the town. Johnny Rose produced a bottle of brandy from somewhere and surreptitiously shared it with Abel as they crouched over a small fire.

'Johnny, I don't know how you do it. You're a rogue, but you're also a life saver.'

Johnny grinned through his dirt encrusted, bearded features. 'One man's loss is another's gain, Abe. Anyway, it's you that's the life saver. I still owe you for stopping me from being knocked off that mountain by a bloody bullock cart.'

'I thank 'ee anyway,' Abel said. 'Now, when are we going to get some bread and meat? I'm starved!'

After resting for two days, the great mass of men, horses, wagons and carts, decamped; and with snow deadening the sound of their movements, they progressed toward Sahagun.

Learning that the French were closing in on them, men began to pay attention to their equipment and weapons, but instead of joining the old enemy in battle, they were suddenly ordered in to a headlong retreat when scouting parties reported that they were facing greatly superior numbers.

Forced marches were endured, swollen rivers crossed and mountain passes negotiated as they strived with might and main to stay ahead of their pursuers. Those who couldn't keep up were left to the mercy of the enemy and the elements.

Camped on frozen snow; Abel, bearded and filthier than ever, gripped his musket and slipped to his knees in despair. Looking back along the path they had taken, he could see the dark, unmoving shapes of human beings and animals; either frozen or starved to death. Some of those corpses were soldiers' wives and their children. Tears of anguish trickled down his face.

'We've had it,' he thought. 'None of us will ever see England again.'

But they didn't all die. In fact, most of the army struggled into Lugo.

Once there, Sir John Moore called a halt to the grim retreat. Food and ammunition were waiting in store and the town's strong defensive position offered him the opportunity to rest his exhausted troops.

The thought of a possible battle actually improved the morale of the force. They had become dispirited by the never-ending retreat. Abel was detached enough to reflect upon the strange phenomenon of half dead, starving men, being cheered up by the opportunity to kill or be killed. He wondered if this attitude was some peculiar British trait, or whether all humankind was made so.

General Soult was not keen on throwing his forces against the natural stronghold of Lugo, so the battle was never joined. After resting for three days, the British continued their march towards Corunna and the troop transports that were rumoured to be waiting in harbour to take them ignominiously back to England. They lived on rumour and gossip.

Abel was among the last of the rearguard to leave Lugo.

Although there had been no sign of Soult's army, he covered several miles before losing an uncomfortable feeling between his shoulder blades.

The disastrous expedition to thwart French ambitions on the Spanish Peninsular continued to run true to form – they arrived at Corunna but there were no ships waiting to take them back to England.

Abel found himself resting, along with Johnny and the raggle-taggle remnants of the 50th Foot, in a large warehouse, close to the town's citadel.

Early on the second morning, a tremendous explosion startled them all awake. It was closely followed by another that rocked even their fortress-like building. A blast of air blew the main doors open, allowing a great cloud of dust to swirl in. Shouts of alarm reached their ears as they grabbed their muskets and rushed to the exits.

'The Frenchies are here already. Now we're for it!'

Several officers appeared, some of them still chewing on their breakfast. Colonel Hill called them to order.

'Steady, men, the French are close by, so we've been obliged to blow our powder stores. We don't want to leave it all for them when we go, do we? Our gunners have been ordered to throw their supply wagons over the cliffs. There just won't be any room for them on board the ships.

A voice called out, 'What ships, your honour; 'ave we got to build 'em ourselves?'

The following day, a huge number of transports entered Corunna harbour. Instead of lifting their spirits, however, their arrival deepened the depression that hung over the remnants of

Moore's expeditionary force. Three thousand men dead and gone, and all for nothing!

Abel was one of the hundreds who felt ill at ease. After marching so far and suffering so much; not to mention the lives lost in battles, they were going home with their tails between their legs. He spat contemptuously. What a waste!

The massive task of embarkation began with the loading of the sick and wounded. They were followed by the artillery pieces and the pride of the army; the cavalry.

'Us poor bloody footsloggers are last agin.' Johnny muttered, as men of the 50th Foot viewed the proceedings from a ridge that provided a defensive position above the harbour.

A terrible slaughter of horses and mules was taking place. There was only enough room on the ships for prime stock, so dozens of animals were being shot or put to the sword by weeping cavalrymen. Their carcasses were sent plummeting into the sea where huge flocks of sea birds gathered to feed on them.

While this saddest of orders was being carried out, other men strove at various, galling, destructive tasks, brought about by - well, they couldn't have explained it if you'd asked them.

Three glory hunting French divisions formed up in spectacular fashion, high above the valley that separated them from the British lines. Convinced that they would at last annihilate what was left of General Moore's Expeditionary Force, they made ready to attack.

Adrenalin began to flow as the British infantry deployed, with the 50th holding the centre.

'Here we go, boys, the odds are in our favour- there's only

about five Frenchies each!'

Men cradled their muskets and wiped bleary faces that were scorched and blackened by long exposure to the elements. Johnny nudged Abel as he looked towards twenty thousand Frenchmen massed on the other side of the valley.

'Look who that is, Abe!'

General Moore was riding grandly along the ridge together with Major Napier. Without an order being given, men of the 50th came to attention; some calling out encouragement to the officers who acknowledged them with casual salutes.

Shortly after that, the French artillery opened fire on them from their hilltop positions a thousand yards away; their lines instantly disappearing behind dense clouds of smoke. Round shot came carving its way through the British at almost the same moment as the sound of the cannon's roar reached them. With their artillery pieces already aboard ship, they had no response.

There was blood of course; blood and torn and severed limbs. Abel's own flesh jumped and tightened in anticipation of pain and death. Screams of agony mingled with cries of defiance as the acrid smell of gunpowder and the sweat of hundreds of unwashed men tainted the air.

The barrage stopped and the smoke dissipated, enabling Abel to see that the French infantry were beginning to descend the rocky slopes, heading for the deserted village below.

British officers started to bawl orders.

'Let's get at 'em, men! Off we go, but keep in line,'

Over the edge went the 50[th.] Click, click, click; on went the bayonets, glittering in menacing rows of sharpened steel.

The entire regiment began to run at the enemy; leaping over fallen branches and small boulders while yelling at the tops of their voices. Hand to hand work being preferable to helplessly accepting volleys of cannon and musket fire, they were desperate to get to grips with Monsoor Crapaud.

A soldier next to Abel stumbled on the rough ground. He shot out an arm to prevent the man from falling over and getting trampled underfoot in the headlong rush. The 50th were heading for a huddle of buildings that were already occupied by scores of French.

Passing the ranks of a cheering regiment that had been ordered to stand fast, Abel was forced on at a furious pace by the press of surrounding men. Glancing quickly round for Johnny, he caught a brief glimpse of his friend's bared teeth and flaring nostrils. His wild eyes were starting from his head. A demon fighter, was Johnny!

The crash of musket fire echoed down the normally peaceful valley.

Then Abel was tearing past the side of a stone building, along with twenty or thirty comrades. Blue and white uniforms loomed up in front of him. Sweat poured down his face as he lunged at a French uniform in time-honoured fashion; feeling the soft impact of steel on flesh. Withdrawing the bayonet, he whirled to meet a threatening blade on his left. Clash of steel on steel. Down went the enemy. Into the throat went Abel's bayonet.

The French began to turn away; heading back to the protection of their artillery.

British officers called out encouragement.

'Forward, men! They're on the run. Keep after them.'

Panting heavily, Abel scrambled among the rocks on the lower slopes of the enemy position. Shattering musket fire poured down from above. As men died to the left and right of him, chips of stone ricocheted into his cheek, drawing blood. Shot and shell from both flanks, as well as from above, was now being poured into the halted British battalion. Death was waiting for anyone foolish enough to attempt to climb that slope. The French had depressed their cannon, making the area a killing field.

Someone yelled above the din.
'Where's the bloody 42nd?'
The cry was taken up. 'Where's the bloody 42nd?'

The distinguished figure of Major Napier stood a few yards from where Abel crouched. He was on foot, red in the face and brandishing his sword. He jumped on to a low wall and, paying no attention to the withering enemy fire, stood upright, waving his hat.

'Come on, the dirty half-hundred! We must take those French guns! Do it for England, men! Don't let's be bested! Oh, the dishonour!'

Abel found himself moving toward the officer. Others were doing likewise. Twenty or so brave hearts were rallying to his call.

'Come on, lads. You gallant boys. Follow me!'

Cheering wildly, they were off; scrambling upwards, trying to hang on to their muskets. To Abel's tired brain it was a nightmare kaleidoscope of colour, noise and pungent smells.

Halfway up the steep ascent, he became aware that men were falling all around him. His mind cleared. He was still close to Napier, but there were no more than six or seven British uniforms on view, and dozens of French were slipping and sliding their way towards them, bayonets at the ready.

'We'll cut our way through, men!' Napier's cry was hoarse but full of fight.

Abel was suddenly filled with the odd conviction that he would not die there. It was inexplicable, but he knew it.

Napier led the little group in a futile attempt to break through the French soldiers now surrounding them.

With his musket gripped firmly in both hands, Abel ploughed headlong into the enemy. He no longer felt human. He didn't know it, but his face was contorted and he was snarling like a wild beast as he used the butt of his musket, his boots and his bayonet to smash, club and stab his way forward, hardly feeling the warm, piercing sensations in various parts of his body. Men fell away from his furious onslaught. A severe blow on the side of his head made him stagger and almost fall.

Suddenly, Abel was on clear ground near the foot of the slope and racing away, roaring like an enraged bull.

A ragged volley of musketry was followed by the zip! zip! of musket balls passing too close for comfort. He felt a burning pain in his side, then heard British voices cheering him on as he made his mad dash.

A few yards more and Abel fell gratefully into the arms of men of the 42nd. They had arrived on the scene too late to provide support for what was left of the 50th.

'Easy, mate, you're 'ome and dry now,' a battered but kindly face looked down on Abel as he sprawled on his back, covered in dust, sweat and blood.

'Where were you 42nd boys?' He panted. 'We could have taken that ridge with a bit o' help.'
'Why, we were doing as ordered and standing fast, lad. We was told we'd been relieved by the guards.'
'Where the bloody hell are they, then?'
'Don't ask me, friend, I only does what I'm told, same as you.'

Musket fire still rattled and rolled around the valley. Abel's head was swimming. 'Where's the 50th, or what's left of 'em?'

'They're falling back over there - out of ball, I expect. Hello, there go the guards now.'

Abel struggled to his feet. 'I must get back.'

'Keep your 'ead down, then,' advised the amiable private. 'It's a bloody miracle you're still in the land o' the living as it is.'

Barely conscious, Abel scrambled from rock to rock, taking advantage of the scant cover available to him. He noted that the French still retained the opposing heights, their batteries still pounding away. 'There goes somebody's home,' he thought, as iron smashed a village hovel to pieces.

After what seemed an eternity, he arrived among familiar faces. Friends came out to assist him. Something odd was happening, though. His legs no longer wanted to support his weight, and a thick mist was hindering his vision. Quite suddenly, all his senses failed him.

Abel was bouncing gently along. Up, down, up, down; he attempted to raise an arm to rub his eyes and found he couldn't.

He managed to speak three words through parched lips.

'What's going on?'

Someone poured water into his mouth, half choking him. Then he heard the familiar voice of Johnny Rose.

'It's all right, Abe, you're on a litter. I'm with you. I got permission. The fighting's over, old friend, and guess what? We're embarking for good old England. Oh, and you're a bloody hero!'

'What?' Abel croaked.

'Well, you know- the forlorn hope and all that rot. You're the sole survivor as far as anybody knows. You suffered five wounds while you were busting through them Frenchies like a battering ram.' Johnny laughed quietly. 'You mad fool!'

The litter rocked and swayed along. From the sound of their tread, Abel deduced that its carriers were marching on cobblestones. He could hear the lap of water and smell the sea – the sea – he drifted away.

He regained his senses aboard HMS Steadfast. A florid little doctor was bending over him as he lay below decks, among fifty or sixty other wounded men.

'Clean wounds, young man. You've suffered severe loss of blood, of course; but you'll do very well if there's no infection. Take plenty of liquids- and I don't mean spirits.'

The doctor turned away to examine the pallid looking individual lying close to Abel.

'This hand might have to come off, you brave fellow. We'll see, we'll see.'

Captain Deane, of whom Abel had only the briefest acquaintance, threaded his way to his cot; crouching to avoid striking his blonde head on the low deck beams.

Abel surprised himself by succeeding in sitting almost upright. Deane proffered a hand. Somewhat taken aback, Abel briefly clasped it. 'Well done, Garnett. I'm glad your wounds are not too serious. You performed bravely and acted in the finest traditions of the regiment. You're the sole survivor of what, considering how you were outnumbered, really was, in this instance, a forlorn hope.'

'Is Major Napier dead, sir?'

'Dead or captive; we're not sure, as yet. Our most grievous loss is General Moore. A great man, indeed. All of England will mourn his death.'

'We've lost the general?'

'I'm afraid so.'

'Did we win the day in the end, sir?'

'Well, we managed to get the bulk of the force away. I suppose one could call it a victory if one counts the number of dead. The French lost two or three thousand to our seven or eight hundred. The gallant 50th took the brunt of it; losing upwards of two hundred men. I'll miss my good friends, Ensign Dixon and Captain Stewart. Did you know them?'

Captain Deane was surprisingly free of class prejudice.

'Well, I knew of them, sir, but that's all. I'm sorry for both them and the regiment.'

'You are a very courageous fellow, Garnett, and when you're fit for duties you will be made sergeant. Having lost five in the battle, we have need of them. I've asked the doctors to take particular care over you. Thank you for setting such a fine example to the men. If you will excuse me, I have to attend my duties.'

The captain returned to a companion way that apparently led from the noisome hold, out into the fresh sea air.

After some tiresome delays, HMS Steadfast finally began corkscrewing its way across the Bay of Biscay, and five days into the voyage, Abel was fit enough to be helped on to the crowded deck to gain a sighting of the English coast.

5

If I had a 'Certain Something' it wasn't obvious to me!

Hard work, they say, doesn't kill people; perhaps not; but years of virtual slave labour and penury certainly do.

Here's a tragic tale; one of the many that remain unrecorded in the world. It concerns my mother.

Anne Elizabeth Lown was born in a workhouse in Kensington, London, in 1907. Her birth certificate states that her father worked as a 'horse handler'. On her 1932 marriage certificate he is described as being a motor mechanic (deceased). Intense research on my part has failed to reveal how and when he died. He simply disappeared. It is a family mystery that mother never spoke about. Did he change his name, abandon his wife and children or simply get sucked into the maelstrom of the First World War?

My mother had a brother. He was killed at Al Alamein in 1942 while serving as a sergeant in the Royal Army Service Corps.

Left on her own, my maternal grandmother moved to a tiny cottage in East Peckham in Kent, where she promptly fell down a flight of stairs and broke her neck. Paralysed and bedridden, she lived for several years in an upstairs room of a dedicated relative's house.

Mother lived a life of endless, small sacrifices. She desperately wanted, and indeed, needed, a daughter, but had five sons and loved a nomadic husband.

She died young, before I was in a position to provide her with a few home comforts. Do I feel any guilt? Don't ask silly questions.

In 1956, I was fifteen years old and, although I was deeply disillusioned with technical school education, thanks to my English teacher, the bright prospect of becoming a journalist loomed large. I could actually be working for a newspaper in nine months!

With that in mind, I stopped attending school and became an office boy, working for Berry & Berry, a firm of solicitors in Tunbridge Wells. They paid for my season ticket from Etchingham and gave me thirty seven shillings and sixpence per week. Sadly, the job turned out to be even more temporary than I'd planned.

Wearing the most ill-fitting suit one can imagine, I travelled to and from work with my head buried in a book to avoid looking at the better dressed commuters.

Berry & Berry were housed in a tall, thin, Victorian building in Church Road. They employed some lovely typists and two or three motherly secretaries. The only other males working there were the three partners. They wore their pinstriped suits as though they were uniforms; imperiously issuing me orders from on high.

Oh, those girls in their summer dresses!

That saucy, young minx, Judy, the switchboard operator, seemed incapable of keeping the top buttons of her blouse fastened. She unfastened even more of them to 'catch the sun' when we lunched together in the garden at the back of the office building. Her artful teasing made it impossible for me to concentrate on reading Nordhoff and **Hall's Mutiny on the Bounty.

I would do my best to keep my eyes fastened on the pages of the book, but I was only human, and didn't she know it! She also knew that I was straight out of school and no danger to anyone.

Along with her best friend, Ann, she loved to sing:

'We are the Queen Street good girls, are we!
We took no pride in our virginity,
So, if it's only good for key holes
And little girlies pee-holes,
It's no good for the Queen Street girls!'

Young, attractive, vivacious; I do hope they didn't settle for a mundane life.

I mastered the complexities of the Still Photography machine, a precursor to photocopiers; reproducing official documents by the score, and took my turn on the antiquated switchboard in Reception. Umpteen buzzers all in a row!

It was full summer, so delivering urgent documents on foot to estate agents and other solicitors' offices all over town, was very pleasurable. It also meant that I was able to visit the public library whenever I wanted to.

Another little pleasure was to be found in taking the staff's cake orders every morning and nipping round the corner to the Cadena Café to buy them in time for the coffee break. I sometimes found myself on the receiving end of a close cuddle for doing that.

'Thank you, Terry, you are sweet.'
'No- thank you, ladies. It was my pleasure!'

Perfume, soft bosoms exuding warmth, and – well, if you've been the least bit lucky in your life, those of you of the male persuasion will remember what that was like when you were young.

Tell the truth and shame the devil? This is my truth.

You may consider me to be way off course here, a lot of people do, you know; but my unfailingly romantic approach to life has me believing that the opposite sex were once the 'ordinary' mans' natural comforters and providers of succour as they struggled through life. Holding the higher moral ground, they were superior to men in most respects; creating, nurturing, consoling and healing. Girls like Judy and Ann were what were known as 'sauce boxes' having harmless fun. They never used foul language, drank mostly 'Babycham', a popular drink with the girls, and only went as far as indulging in heavy petting with the chosen few. In recent years, too many of these once superior beings have become hardheaded. Bullet-headed, too, some of them; more inclined to be killers on the front line than they are to nurse the wounded and comfort the dying soldier. Seemingly unconcerned about the loss, young females throw away their natural grace and beauty along with their modesty, if they were ever brought up to have any, as they shriek, swear, drink to excess-and- well, the plethora of salacious television programmers available to the youth of today, and no doubt, tomorrow, should point you in the right direction. To complete this little tirade from a Neanderthal: what has feminism, 'equality' and equal opportunity actually been a major contributor to? Oh, nothing very important; just the breakdown of family life, to the detriment of a stable, civilised society. Having degraded themselves to the level of men the fairer sex threw out the baby with the bathwater.

Then again; I am not in favour of women being suborned into becoming passive Stepford Wives, either. I'm all for balance.

While betrayal is rife on both sides of the marriage bed in today's world, true love and faithfulness prevails in my fortunate life, so I can only imagine how I'd feel if it happened to me.

Bitter Winds

'When 'ere the bitter winds of loneliness doth blow
I main recall the vow of loyalty thee trow.
With downy quilts clutched to my solitary frame,
I make fervent wish that their caress was thine.

Alack, the wraps will not at my behest
Become the barest simulation of thy breast,
Nor provide a hint of scented hair
Or yield like living flesh that tender hands explore.
Oh! Where are the soft enfolds of your embrace?
Gone! Gone to another's bed-chambered place,
Wherein your modesties become unlaced.

Come Morpheus, the merciful, and ease my heart.
Give me those dulcie dreams in which we never part,
But lie entwined as one in loving sleep,
Until we wake and plight our troth to keep.

Well, it's better than simply saying, 'She's buggered off with somebody else,' don't you think?

Meanwhile, back at the ranch, disaster struck. In September

1956, my father decided to 'up-sticks' from Hurst Green. He had somehow managed to obtain work on a farm in faraway Wiltshire. Protesting that Mr. Parsons was going to take me on as a reporter on one of his newspapers when I became sixteen, was a useless exercise; and shouting matches only upset the rest of the family, especially my mother.

I considered staying on in Tunbridge Wells. I was day dreaming, of course. Even if Berry and Berry added the cost of my train fare to my cash wagers, the total would still be nothing like enough to pay for bed and board in the cheapest hostel available.

So away we went to darkest Wiltshire.

The girls at Berry & Berry were very kind to me. On the day I left, they presented me with two books: Willi Heinrich's 'The Willing Flesh' (an ironic title under the circumstances) and Jerome K Jerome's 'Three Men in a Boat'.

After we arrived in Wiltshire: muddy lane, cottage in the middle of nowhere; an uncontrollable and undoubtedly heartless urge came over me. While reading the 'Situations Vacant' columns in the county newspaper, I saw that the 'Old Bell' hotel in Warminster was advertising for a 'live-in kitchen boy'.

My application for the position was successful.

Without saying goodbye to anyone and racked with guilt about leaving my ailing mother and my two younger brothers, I stuffed what possessions I had into a cheap suitcase and left the cottage.

Putting all thoughts of a career in journalism out of my mind, I made my way to Warminster and entered an environment that was completely alien to any I had yet known. I was a stranger in a strange land, all right.

Mr. and Mrs. Stewart, the managers of the former coaching inn, which still retained a great deal of old world charm, were very kind to me. They also proved to be extremely tolerant about my misdeeds and acts of sheer stupidity.

My job meant that I had to be 'first up' every morning so that I could stoke the boiler and light the kitchen stoves before the breakfast chef came down from his room. During the day, I could be found carrying guests' luggage, running errands in town, helping the kitchen staff prepare food, taking care of deliveries- and a lot more besides. I had my own room in the staff corridor, was allowed to eat three meals a day and received £3 per week, plus tips. Apart from the worm of guilt in my mind, I was in clover!

.

I had no knowledge of the world, or the people in it; apart from that which I'd garnered from reading novels written by the likes of Dickens, Anthony **Hope, GA Henty, Leslie Charteris, Dornford Yates, etc, along with the volumes my mother had borrowed from mobile libraries. Reading her choice of books did nothing to straighten my skewed, out of date, perception of life; far from it. Lord Peter Wimsey and Hercule Poirot were no more representative of ordinary people than Rudolf Rassendyll, the Saint, the Berry family or Peterkin of 'The Coral Island'. So there I was, in late 1956, a chivalrous, well-mannered, naïve boy, in his first real job, and ready to kick authority figures, such as head waiters, in the seat of their pants whenever they displayed a lack of gallantry towards the opposite sex; all of whom I had stuck high on a pedestal.

The hotel was full of young, and not so young, females. Waitresses and chambermaids, a couple of glamorous receptionists, and nubile girls arriving with their parents- I simply loved carrying their suitcases for them!.

I had only worked there for a few weeks when the first of several incidents occurred for which I should have suffered instant dismissal.

Sackable offence, number one:

The blood rushed to my besotted, unworldly brain one busy evening when Ernest, the head waiter, kicked the object of my desire, a pretty young waitress, up the rear, in order to hurry her up. How dare he mistreat the love of my life!? Dropping whatever it was I was doing, I rushed around the huge kitchen table and, watched by two chefs and the old boy in the pot-wash, gave him the same treatment just as he was disappearing through the swing doors leading to the dining room. He was carrying an order of Sole Colbert on a stainless steel platter. The impact of my foot on his black-tailed backside sent him sprawling, causing a certain amount of consternation among the customers. The Dover Sole made a valiant attempt to become a flying fish, but Ernest had a firm thumb grip on its tail fin, so it remained neatly on the salver at the end of his outstretched arm. The parsley-butter and lemon garnish, however, made good their escape; vanishing beneath an overhanging tablecloth.

That love of my life, the abused but unruffled young waitress, helped Ernest to his feet, while I, with honour satisfied, but believing I was 'done for', stood quaking in my boots in the doorway.

I was saved by the fact that, although he was most definitely a misogynist, Ernest was a decent chap. All I got from him was a lot of threats and finger wagging.

Not long after that incident, the upwardly mobile waitress threw me over for a lad with a motorbike. He turned up outside a youth club where I had a date with the girl in question.

'You don't mind if I go for a little ride on the back of his motorbike, do you, Terry?'

I did, of course, but said that I didn't. The little hussy straddled the pillion seat and off they went.

Like the fool I was, I waited for her- and waited for her. She didn't come back.

A recipe for Sole Colbert:

Skin a whole Dover Sole. Dip it in seasoned flour, beaten eggs and fine breadcrumbs. Pan-fry the fish and carefully remove its backbone. Fill the resulting cavity with *Maitre d' Hotel butter. Add a little meat glaze. Serve on a dish garnished with lemon butterflies and parsley.

*Mix chopped parsley, lemon juice and finely chopped spring onions with butter. Form a cylinder with the mixture and freeze it. Cut it in to roundels before using it as a garnish for the fish.

Sackable offence, number two:

I managed to set fire to my bed.

Kitchen and Waiting staff may have been at loggerheads during service times, but peace reigned between them when work was over. We played card games late into the night, drinking and smoking ourselves to death as we did so.

After one such session, I crawled onto my bed, lay down fully dressed and fell instantly asleep while smoking a cigarette. By the time I woke up, it had fallen from my hand, burnt a hole through the bedding and dropped inside the mattress. Part of its flock interior was already glowing and the room was beginning to fill with smoke.

Panic Stations!

After my first feeble attempts to extinguish the fire failed miserably, I had a brainwave. Acting upon it, I dragged the smouldering mattress from the room, along the staff corridor and in to the bathroom at the end of it. Not one member of staff opened their door to find out what the hell was going on at two o' clock in the morning. They too had gone to bed 'smashed'.

Squashing the mattress into the bath, I turned on the taps. Water won the battle, but the mattress would never see a bed again. On top of that, the bathroom, the corridor, and my bedroom were all in a mess.

Came the dawn-came Mr. Stewart, the hotel manager.

'We'll have to get you another mattress and some new bedding, Terry,' he said.

Not one word of criticism escaped his lips. In fact, quite amazingly, soon after my sixteenth birthday I found myself promoted to commis chef. Proudly wearing a toque, I made omelettes, carved joints of meat and began to learn how to turn raw ingredients into attractive, edible comestibles.

Sackable offence, number three

Our new head chef liked a drink, but he didn't like me. Given my impudent attitude towards him, I can't say I blame him. One busy evening, with the second chef off sick, I found myself resentfully working alone with him. When a waitress told the chef that a customer had complained about his 'Rognons Turbigo', I piped up with a crass, insulting remark.

'Well, it didn't look right to me, either,' or something like that.

'RIGHT!' the chef exploded, 'If you think you can do better, now's your chance!'

He barged his way out of the kitchen, went to his room and packed his suitcases. Without speaking a further word to anyone, he was out of the hotel in ten minutes flat; leaving me with a host of orders to cope with.

Panic Stations!

Mr. and Mrs. Stewart saved the day; they knew their way round a commercial kitchen, and the waiting staff saved my bacon. None of them mentioned the insulting remark I had made to the chef; they simply reported that he'd stormed out after receiving a complaint from a customer. Thank you, Ernest; thank you, girls.

I would provide you with a complete recipe for Rognons Turbigo, but you will not prepare it, will you?. Few people, other than the rich, who consume jazzed up, high-priced versions of it in Michelin-starred restaurants, eat offal, nowadays. Stuffed sheep's' hearts, sautéed chicken livers, braised ox tongue, pigs' trotters? Not too many people choose to eat what used to be the ingredients of 'Humble Pie', nowadays.

Suffice to say that Kidneys' Turbigo consists of sautéed kidneys in a rich sauce, together with button onions and chipolata sausages, garnished with large croutons of fried bread, their corners dipped in chopped parsley.

Panic Stations!

The management were going on holiday. Would I be kind enough to look after their budgerigar while they were away? I could keep it in my room.

They handed me the caged bird on the day of their departure. I duly took it to my room, feeling sorry for the poor little thing sitting on its perch. Before the Stewart's car had left the hotel yard, I decided to give the budgerigar the freedom of my room. I did more than that, I gave it the whole world, because I hadn't completely closed the window! It made a bee-line for the small aperture, went through it-and disappeared over the rooftops. Having lost their budgerigar immediately after it had been placed in my care, I had to wait for two agonising weeks before I was able to inform the Stewarts.

Due to my background, this wonderful, imperturbable couple had the crazy idea that I was a bit of a handyman. I wasn't. 'Not by as long chalk,' as my father would say.

One or the other of them would button-hole me.

'Oh, Terry, the people in room eleven are having a bit of trouble with their gas fire. Be a dear and go and have a look at it for me, will you?'

'Pop down to the boiler room, Terry, and see what's going on. The water's running cold again.'

I managed to avoid blowing up the hotel.

With their faith in me seemingly undimmed, the Stewart's asked me to renovate an old, 'sit up and beg', bike they had in their garage. They wanted to surprise their son with it.

I took it to pieces, added a new chain, drop handlebars and derailleur gears; the last giving me no end of trouble, then oiled every movable part and painted its frame- sort of.

Watching their son, Charles, riding it round and round the hotel yard, they thanked me profusely; seemingly blind to the fact that the paint work was probably the worst ever seen on a bicycle, or indeed, in the history of painting in general.

They even gave an old school friend of mine a job, on my recommendation!

I had been writing to Barry ever since I had somewhat precipitately left Bexhill Tech, where we had become firm friends. He had suffered a traumatic early childhood and after leaving school at the first opportunity, had joined an Army Apprentice School.

It transpired that Barry and the army didn't see eye to eye, so they parted company after a year.

I began receiving worrying letters from him, describing what seemed to be the dissolute life he was leading in Deptford, south east London. Feeling that I had to get him out of there, I approached my amiable bosses and they very obligingly gave him the job I'd been doing before I became one of the chefs.

Barry arrived at the hotel like a courier bearing news of the outside world. Unlike me, he had all that was required to be part of the revolutionary youth culture that was beginning to take over Britain in 1957; the haircut, the clothes and fantastic knowledge of the modern music scene. He could do a great impression of Cliff Richard and placed a permanent order with the newsagent's opposite the hotel for any new Elvis Presley record that became available. It was the only way in which one could buy a record in Warminster in those days. It did have a coffee bar with a juke box, though. Suddenly, they were all the rage.

Sometime during this period I enjoyed my first visit to a theatre. The wit of George Bernard **Shaw's, The Doctor's Dilemma, was a revelation as big as Olivier's performance in the film Richard the Third had been.

Together, Barry and I got up to juvenile mischief, drunk rather too much alcohol and did our best with the girls who came our way.

Patricia was a New Zealander on an extended working holiday. She was about four years older than I was when she became a temporary waitress at the hotel.

It wasn't long before I found myself accompanying her on bike rides, usually to Longleat Estate where there were plenty of secluded spots to dally in. It was a brief, inconclusive romance. Before she moved on, Patricia gave me a few packs of cigarettes and a note which read, quite simply.

'Think of me as you smoke every fourth one, Terry.'

One might forget some of the things that happened a lifetime ago, but one never forgets details about early romantic encounters. They stay clear in one's' mind.

It can hardly have been due to my good looks and sophistication, but after Patricia's departure, I became briefly involved with an attractive, married lady, aged about twenty five. Put aside all thoughts that I may be about to begin bragging about this, because I'm not. I was a fool out of my depth and I respect her memory as much as I do Patricia's.

Let's call her- 'Amy', she worked as a part-time waitress.

It began when she told me she was nervous about walking home alone at night, after finishing work. I told her that I would escort her, of course. It was the decent thing to do.

Panic Stations!

What wasn't the decent thing for me to do was to respond when she began flirting, then kissing me as we walked the dark footpaths to her house on the outskirts of Warminster; but I was nearly seventeen by then, and testosterone was running my life.

Arriving separately, we would meet each other in the back row of the local cinema on our afternoon's off; or in the wooded areas of the local park. In retrospect I realise that the perfectly nice 'Amy' must have been neglected at home and was also trying to cling on to the heady days of her recent youth. Sordid? Perhaps it was, but our yearnings had a kind of heart-rending beauty about them. My own innocence was not quite lost and Amy's could never be regained. 'Blue Remembered Hills' all over the place.

Inevitably, my conscience started to nag. I'm not sure whether they make cowards of us all; but mine certainly drove me away from Warminster- and 'Amy'.

Sadly, I was too naïve and inexperienced to handle our parting in a fittingly adult manner.

'Amy'

'Escorting Amy closely homeward,
Through clover newly mown,
Under the rhododendron blooms,
She demurred from lying down.
The blouse ribbon at her throat, though,
I was empowered to untie;
Consequently causing a sigh.

The last time I saw Amy,
With her tender hands touching me,
Her lips and her eyes begged an, 'always,
Always think well of me,' plea.
I failed to say, 'Amy, darling,
You'll have a place in my heart 'til I die.'
Subsequently causing a sigh.

Days slid one to another.
Innocence became debased.
I found myself tearing at more tawdry clothes
Than the blouse that I once unlaced.
But fortunate men find
A 'Marriage d' Amour',
Some fortunate as I.
Constantly causing a sigh.'

In a bit of an emotional turmoil, I secured a job as a second chef at a hotel in Essex.

Soon after I arrived there the hotel kitchen was struck by lightning! Was God after me for committing a sin?

A large and ancient cauldron standing in an open fireplace was split asunder, all the lights in the hotel went out and flood water began entering the packed dining room. Everyone was ushered upstairs to the first floor for a while.

A couple of days later the national press published photographs of the flooded town, including one showing a man paddling a canoe between the counters in Woolworths.

I heard from Barry. He had moved on and become a waiter at a country club near Cheltenham. Whilst there, he met and fell in love with the daughter of wealthy parents. When mater and pater broke the relationship up, Barry, not yet eighteen years old, made his way to Bristol and joined the Merchant Navy. In no time at all he was on a cargo ship bound for South America. Bravo, Barry!

The chef was having an affair with a waitress, so I became his messenger boy, taking notes to his wife, informing her that he was too busy to come home for the afternoon, or he had a buffet to prepare, etc. I hadn't read The Go-Between at the time. If I had done so, I would have inevitably romanticised my involvement, making the whole thing more acceptable to me. By the way, I'm well ahead of you on this one; it's a thing of beauty when I dally with a married woman, but something altogether different when a married man is unfaithful to his wife. The past certainly is another country, all right.

I spent a lot of time in cinemas; falling in love with the likes of Ruth Roman, Janet Leigh and the sultry Ursula **Thiess. When I wasn't doing that, I was sitting alone in a coffee bar on my afternoons off, miserably contemplating the fact that, unlike my brothers, Mick and Owen, I would not be required to do National Service. Between them, they had served in Egypt, Korea, Germany, Libya and Gibraltar, and I had never set foot on a foreign shore! Having missed the last call-up deadline by a few weeks, I decided to enlist; sticking to my decision even when the grateful chef told me that, as a reward for services rendered, he could get me a job in the galley aboard Lord and Lady Docker's yacht, Shemara. It had been rented out to the Van de Burgh's, the Stork margarine people, for a year, and was going on a world cruise. Who knows what roads I would have walked down if I had taken that job?

6

Good and Evil

Our entire universe, and no doubt, countless other universes, are maintained by a multiplicity of positives and negatives. It doesn't take too much imagination for one to realise that their endless fight for supremacy extends to the battle between good and evil in mankind. Not only that; it is quite obvious that evil enjoys many victories.

'There {probably} are more things in heaven and earth, Horatio…,'

'The Tethered Goat'

All along the line, our guns were depressed to their lowest elevation, their long, black barrels pointing like so many admonishing fingers to where the German infantry crouched in their water-logged, muddy trenches, awaiting the signal whistles that would impel them towards us across three hundred yards of no-man's land.

I looked on my own battery of gunners with great affection. They stood at their posts, waiting for the command to load.

After interminable delays, my regiment had finally received the very first consignment of war's latest death dealer, the 'Tadcaster' 'airburst' shell. Now it was up to us to demonstrate their effect on the enemy. Exploding at head height, the shells' lethal contents would decimate their ranks, scything them down even more effectively than machine guns, or so the trials had demonstrated.

The sound of distant whistles galvanized me.

'Here they come!

'Load!'
'Load!
'Load!'

My voice mingled with those of the other battery commanders as a great phalanx of grey-uniformed figures hauled themselves into view and began a determined approach.

Leaning forwards, they moved like automatons, crossing the shattered landscape. It was easy for me to imagine how tightly they gripped their weapons, because my own hand clutched my service revolver like a vice.

Our teams of accomplished gunners went swiftly through the loading procedure.

'Ready!'
'Ready!'
'Ready!'

'Fire!'
'Fire!'
'Fire!

My shouted orders combined with those of the other officers. .
The Germans were running at us now. Two hundred yards!
Sergeants began bawling at their gun teams.
'Stand away!'

'Gun jammed!'

'Gun jammed!'
No shell bursts. No charnel house out on the wasteland, just a silence broken only by the battle cries emanating from the

mouths of five thousand rapidly approaching enemy soldiers.

Our machine gunners and riflemen opened up a fierce fusillade. One thought stood clear in my mind. 'I must clear the breech in that nearest gun! Do my duty as an officer.'

But as I approached the impotent artillery piece, a great noise blasted me into nothingness. My last thought was, 'the Hun is upon us!'

I burst back into the living world in something of a panic, blinking and perspiring. My eyes focused on Nurse Hazell as, not for the first time, she wiped the visible parts of my face with a cool and soothing flannel.

'Having another bad dream, Lieutenant Gorman, sir? Never mind. Your bandages come off today. You'll feel better after that. You're a lucky man, sir. Doctor Philmore told me you are one of only thirteen survivors in your sector.

I licked my dry lips and croaked, 'thirteen out of two hundred and seventy? Oh, God!'

'I reckon it were God that saved you, sir,' Nurse Baxter said. 'Doctor Philmore says that about half of them poor devils got blown up, just like you did, when our own guns exploded. There's something terribly wrong somewhere when things like that happen; still, just think how lucky you are, sir. You'll soon be home with your family.'

****

I was hiking along a hot and dusty lane in Elgar country. Solitude and the English summer countryside were restoring me. The soothing streams running through rolling, green meadows in the shadow of the hills around Malvern were in sharp contrast to the dusty road I trod, under an overheated sun. Easing the weight of the pack on my back, I mopped my brow, touching the pulsing scar on the side of my head as I did so. The more the sun beat down on me the more painful the wound became.

I trudged on for a little while longer, bowing beneath that fiery furnace and thinking, 'this is not right. The sun just doesn't get this hot!' My head hurt like never before.. Was I becoming ill again?'

Due to the white glare that blinded me wherever I looked, I came upon the tavern before realising it was there.

The building was long, dark and low; so low in fact, that, as I made my way to its entrance, my aching head almost struck the sign suspended by iron chains from a beam of wood. It depicted what appeared to be a half-crazed Billy goat tied to the base of a gibbet. A great, pink tongue hung down over the animal's matted beard and its red eyes blazed in their sockets. The sign informed me that I was at the 'Tethered Goat'.

I didn't care for that inn sign very much, but my one thought was to get inside, away from the extraordinary heat. Perhaps the landlord would allow me to bathe my face in some cool water.

The gloomy room I entered was as malodorous as any mud-filled, front line trench, replete with rat-gnawed corpses. I almost gagged; covering my mouth with the kerchief I had been using to wipe away sweat. 'What sort of a drinking establishment is this?'

I thought at first that the place was deserted until I saw the back of a very tall man, standing behind the bar. Head down, he turned to face me and began tapping a long finger on the counter.

'Drink?' He queried, speaking into his tangled beard as I came closer to him. This mundane question was asked in a remarkably sinister and menacing tone.

'A pint of cider, if you please,' I responded, adding, 'can't you let some fresh air into this place?'

He slowly lifted his head, raised two large hands and pushed a tangled mess of grey hair away from his eyes. I saw his face for the first time- and quailed before it. The man's features were not human; they were a replica of the goat on the sign outside. The heat left my body as though I had been suddenly plunged in to ice-water. This was nightmare of a different kind. I could not believe that elongated jaw, the slash of mouth with a curling, saliva dripping tongue hanging from it. A succession of shudders passed through me. The creature's' unspeakable eyes, red-rimmed, and black with evil, turned fully upon me. The pain in my head became too much to bear.

'Somebody help me!' The words escaped from my lips as, without any noticeable movement, he, or it, was suddenly looming over me and reaching out with those great hands! Utter terror! I pulled a scouts' knife from my belt; the one I had owned since my schooldays and had brought with me on a sentimental whim. As fingers of steel fastened upon my throat, I lashed out with it, stabbing and stabbing at the thing's upper body and feeling an enormous sense of elation as it began to spurt blood and emit screams of anguish. It was mortal then! Then a human, mustachioed face, twisted in agony, emerged from that of the creatures. My knife was suddenly plunging into a tweed--jacketed torso. The pain in my head increased to such a degree that, for the second time in my recent life, the world swam away from me. I was lost to darkness.

The London News.
September 11th. 1918

'Young officer, crazed by war experiences,
Guilty of killing famous industrialist.'

Royal Artillery officer, Lieutenant Harold Lucas Gorman, aged 26, arrested last month for the murder of Lord Tadcaster, has been found guilty but insane and has been committed to a secure mental institution for an indefinite period.

We can now reveal that when he was discovered at the scene of the crime by two of Lord Tadcaster's gamekeepers, Lieutenant Gorman was covered in blood and had fainted away. Upon being revived, he insisted that he had been attacked by what he described as 'a demon' in a hostelry called the 'Tethered Goat'. Needless to say there is no such establishment of that peculiar name in the district.

Psychologist, Dr Grayson Phillips, has deduced that the unfortunate officer became deranged after receiving a serious head wound during the notorious, 'Tadcaster Shell' incident at Boissy when his regiment, the 117th. Light Artillery, was almost wiped out to a man due to a faulty consignment of the new projectiles which were produced in Lord Tadcaster's munitions factories.

Having demonised Lord Tadcaster in his own mind, Lieutenant Gorman had sought his lordship out and murdered him near his home in the Malvern Hills. Tragically, Lord Tadcaster, 52, lost his wife, Lady Margaret, and his daughter, Isobel, in the recent influenza epidemic.

They come to me in the dark of my cell and the terror of it has made me gaunt and pale. There is no understanding or humanity in my unbelieving keepers. The lesser ones laugh at me and call me, 'Screwy', while the doctors make soothing noises.

eep in the night I smell Tadcaster's presence before I hear or see his mewling and increasingly corrupt form. Black blood seeps through gashes in the ragged tweed jacket he wears. A piece of decaying flesh falls away from his skull and his empty eye sockets take on a hideous aspect as tears of self pity ooze from them. The gibbering spectre thrusts itself against me,

'Damn you to hell, Gorman! You sent me to him before my time! You will join me sooner or later. I will never stop calling upon him to make you suffer! NEVER!'

The rotting corpse fades from view, leaving me alone in my terror.

Then HE comes. Blubbering, I crawl to the furthest corner of my cell and make myself small, screwing my eyes tight shut. The horned one is there, his vile lips, dripping slime, whisper against my ear as his long, bony fingers caress my scarred head.

'I can make you free-e-e-e! Give you riches beyond belief and all the women you can ever use to comfort you during a long, long life. They will be my reward to you if you swear an oath in my name that you will never invoke – the other one…

I find the courage to speak,

'God will destroy you. You are pure evil! He is greater than you.'

A cold hand crushes my nose and mouth so that I cannot breathe. 'DESTROY me? Do you think that I am NOTHING?'

Gobs of spittle slide down my forehead as he chokes with rage. 'I stand as high as the –other one – higher! It was MY war, MY plan, MY finger on the trigger at Sarajevo. The assassin, Princip, was in my hands! And it was ME that addled the General's brains, allowing them to send tons of living, human flesh to be slaughtered by machine guns. My quota of that is now enduring what must be endured for all eternity. Tadcaster's infamous shell was just an amusing diversion for me. One of myriads! Guns jammed- then BOOM!'

The fiend laughed a terrible laugh. 'Tadcaster gave me his oath that he would never invoke the other's name. I made him rich and powerful, but he was soon begging HIM to be merciful when his wife and daughter were dying. He broke the black rule and had to pay for it. You were my chosen instrument. I allowed you to live while your comrades died, so that you could use your little knife on Tadcaster and send him to me.'

The voice of evil took on a whimsical, but at the same time, utterly depraved tone.

'I'm as busy as ever. The war may have stopped but I'm quite happy with the results. After all that death and destruction, I have disease, starvation, crippled minds and bodies and a certain Herr Hitler to amuse me. I've still got more than enough time for you, Gorman. There's work for you to do in the world, unless you want to stay in this madhouse.'

When he finally removed his hand from my mouth, the stink of his breath filled my nostrils. His leathery tongue rasped hideously across my face, licking up his own spittle.

'Give me your allegiance now, or rot here until I come again. For I will come, and I will keep coming to you until you are mine!'

I struggle to speak. The words eventually erupting from my mouth,

'God save me! God Save me!'

Snarling like a great wolf, the evil one bared his blackened teeth and snatched up the gobbet of Tadcaster's putrefying flesh from where it had fallen. He thrust it into his gaping maw before disappearing into nothingness, while I screamed out the Lord's name until my unbelieving keepers entered the cell to restrain and sedate me.

Lost Worlds (2)

1

You're on the slide again, Ward!

I never bore witness to the rapid disintegration of the world I grew up in. In addition to the onset of rock and roll and the teenage revolution; the pace of life in the countryside also quickened as the plodding Shire horse was replaced by Ferguson or Fordson tractors. Intensive farming became the order of the day as combine harvesters roared their way up and down the corn fields. Threshing machines and steam engines were reduced to making appearances at agricultural shows. While all this was happening, I was away, playing the smallest of roles in a very different world that was also on the verge of extinction.

By 1958, that force for good in the world, the British Empire, was also disappearing, but the army still retained its great regiments-and the troopships to transport them to all points east. Gibraltar, Cyprus, Aden, East Africa- the Far East; although he might risk his neck from time to time, a regular soldier could travel the world at the taxpayers' expense.

I took a long, lonely walk down Queen's Avenue, Aldershot, on a wet November evening. Having joined the regular army at the youngest permissible age, I was making my way towards the Army Catering Corps barracks where I was to report to the guard room.

Earlier that day, having collected the few possessions I had left at my family's cottage, I had journeyed to Salisbury and walked in to the army recruiting office there.

I passed some basic intelligence tests and chose to become a member of the ACC because I had a little kitchen experience. The recruiting sergeant informed me that I would be sent for in a week or two. Well, I wasn't having that, was I? I had left my job and my family had no idea what I was doing, so I could hardly return home.

'You're not on the run from the law, are you?' the sergeant asked, when I told him I wanted to join the army straight away.

After looking me over; seeing a callow youth scarcely out of short trousers, standing in front of him, he sighed and said,

'All right, lad. I'll make a couple of 'phone calls and see if I can get you up there today.'

I had no idea where 'up there' might be, until he handed me some paperwork and a rail warrant that would take me to Aldershot.

'The orderly room at Clayton Barracks will be closed by the time you get there, so show these to the duty sergeant in the guard room. You can't miss it, it's right by the main gate. Good luck, boy.'

There are many stories about the personal experiences of newly enlisted soldiers and their training, so I will not provide a blow by blow account of how I muddled through and survived. I had my bed turned over, of course; nearly everyone did at one time or other. In my case it was because my toothbrush was shown to still have traces of paste on it while laid out for a kit inspection.

On my second morning in camp I was marched, as one of a cadre of new recruits, to the canteen for breakfast. Ordered to come to a stamping halt on a slippery, sloping roadway, wearing my brand new army boots, I fell over and broke the half-pint mug I had just been issued with. I did it again the next morning, breaking another mug.

'You'll never make a bleedin' soldier, Ward!'

Years later, I met that particular sergeant when I stayed in the SAS camp at Hereford, while I was in transit. I held the same rank that he did by then- but he'd given up one stripe in order to join the elite force. He didn't remember me.

Having passed a butchers' trade test and completed an officers' mess chef's course, I emerged from training with one stripe on my arm. There's glory for you!

Off I went to join the 14th Field Regiment of Artillery. They were based at Barford Camp, near Barnard Castle in County Durham.

I discovered that the camp had its own railway 'Halt' on the Darlington to Barnard Castle line.

Carrying my kit, I alighted there on a blustery March afternoon in 1959 and followed a narrow footpath across a couple of fields; entering the rear of the camp through an unguarded gate.

I found the guard room and reported my presence.

The first thing I saw when I entered a dim, deserted billet, set aside for members of the ACC, was a body hanging by a rope from a cross beam in the centre of the room. It gave me quite a start, but the 'corpse' turned out to be nothing more than the stuffed dummy replica of a cook-sergeant. With a beret set at a jaunty angle on a head formed out of who knew what, it was dressed in a pair of chef's trousers and a battledress complete with three stripes. I discovered later that the thing hung there permanently. No officer or senior NCO ever came near us. The cooks were lepers, as far as 14th Field Regiment was concerned. We were not real soldiers at all! That was odd, because, back in the Aldershot NAAFI, fighting- mad members of the ACC had invariably trounced 2 Para!

Our accommodation was a wooden billet, complete with pot-belly stove, standing on a slope above the cookhouse; well away from the rest of the camp. I was to discover that the RSM didn't want a bunch of scruffy cooks contaminating the real fighting men in his care, or have us messing up any of his parades. Good-oh!

I chose an unoccupied bed at the far end of the billet, an d after stowing my kit in a locker, made it up and stretched out, wondering what life had in store for me.

After a while the door was flung back and a dozen or so, over-excited young cooks crashed through it. Spotting me, they immediately put me to the test. Two of them, like the hooligans they were, charged towards me, intending to give the new bloke a ******* good scragging. What a piece of luck I had! When the first of them lunged at me, I accidentally executed a perfect 'flying mare' on him by raising my feet to fend him off. My nice, shiny boots connected squarely with his chest and his own impetus sent him straight over both me and my bed. Although I tried not to show it, I was as surprised as everyone else when he ended up on the floor in the proverbial crumpled heap. The other threatening character lost interest in giving me a Gorbals welcome and asked me in a thick Scots accent what my name was. That was how I came to be more or less accepted as one of 14th Field Regiment's cooks.

Here they were, as large as life; the traditional band of foul-mouthed, abysmally ignorant, skiving, lecherous, scrounging, conniving soldiers, all crammed together in one billet. As the Duke of Wellington once remarked when he was inspecting his troops, 'I don't know what they do to the enemy, but by God, they frighten me.' And who was in charge of- well, I must say 'us', not 'them', because, not wishing to become a complete outcast, I soon became as degraded as the rest- I'll tell you who was in charge of us; it was a homosexual cook sergeant; the predatory kind. That's why his effigy hung in our billet.

I was warned he would 'try it on' with me, and he did. The first time I encountered him, he felt obliged to 'adjust the length' of my chef's apron. He had his little feel, but that was all he got, because I went to work in the officers' mess, not the cookhouse he presided over.

On one occasion it was necessary for me to take a message to his room. Fortunately, perhaps, he wasn't there when I opened the door, but the lads were right, it did smell like a Chinese brothel, or what we all imagined one would smell like! .

The second in command of 1st Field Battery (The Blazers) was Captain Evans, a very urbane and unpretentious man. He was my messing officer. We got on well; so well in fact that when the time came for 1st Field Battery to undertake a training exercise on the Otterburn Ranges, he ordered me to take care of the catering. I couldn't bring myself to tell him that I had not received any field training and I didn't know one end of a field kitchen from another. In their infinite wisdom, those in charge of things back in Aldershot, had ordered me, and many others like me, to clean the entire camp, instead. The annual 'admin inspection' was due, so even the piles of coal had to be whitewashed. After the inspection was over they had promptly posted me to a field regiment!

The 25 pounder artillery pieces used by 14th Field Regiment, required twenty four men to crew a battery of four guns. They also needed two officers, a sergeant, at least one gun fitter, a couple of royal signalmen, a medic, and REME personnel to maintain the vehicles- about thirty two men in all. Fortunately, the always lucky Lance Corporal Ward, was assigned Private Dagnan to assist him. Dagnan knew much more than I did about using such lethal weapons as No 1 Petrol Burners to cook food with; although, later on, he was to over-reach himself and blow up one of my field kitchens in Aden!

The weather on the bleak Northumberland moors was appalling throughout the entire exercise. Our water bowser was severely battered when it skidded off a road and I thought my last moment had arrived when the prop shaft of the ration truck I was travelling in came adrift while we were tearing down hill towards a narrow bridge. The gunner/driver managed to bring the lorry to a skidding halt before we reached it; after which, we sat there smoking cigarettes to calm our nerves.

The officers and men got fed somehow, and none of them threatened to lynch either Dagnan or myself.

Inglorious moments in Darlington. It was quite amazing how much drink could be purchased with a soldier's weekly pay in 1959. Too much! I was on the slide; downing pints of Strongarm beer, picking up girls in dance halls- having my thumb severely bitten for attempting a little too much exploratory work beneath a nice girl's blouse and having drunken brawls with local lads. It couldn't last, not with my conscience. Wasn't I a cut above the rest of the wild bunch in my billet? I'm afraid I wasn't.

Late one night, while I was staggering along a road in yet another drunken stupor, I was given a lift back to camp by fellow cook, Jim Felton.

The next morning, having recovered my senses, I said to him, 'I didn't know you had a car, Jim.'
'I don't,' he said, 'I nicked it 'cos I missed the last bloody 'bus, same as you did. Well, I wasn't going to walk all the way, was I?'

Picture seven or eight inebriated soldiers hanging on to the outside of a huge Scammel Recovery Vehicle as it careers along country roads in the middle of the night, heading for Barnard Castle; I came close to being scraped off by the low-hanging branches of a tree. Laughing like a buffoon, I clung to the metalwork.

I became involved in a drunken brawl in Darlington; blacked out and came to my senses in more ways than one when I discovered that it was dawn and I was standing in a meadow in the middle of nowhere. Some corner of my mind must have continued functioning while I was 'out', though, because beside the field I so much wanted to curl up and go to sleep in there was a road- it led to Barford Camp.

That old levelling dust of fate came to my rescue. While the rest of the regiment was going to Hong Kong, 1st Field Battery, under the command of Major Bowen and Captain Evans, was being posted to Aden. They needed a cook NCO. Seizing the opportunity to get the hell out of Dodge, I volunteered for the job and was accepted.

To prepare us for the heat of the Aden Protectorate and its desert waste lands, 1st Field Battery was sent on exercise to the snowy Cairngorm Mountains in Scotland!

One of the gunners thought that, because heat rises, he would be warmer if he slept on top of a Bedford lorry's canopy, wrapped in blankets. When he woke up, he forgot where he was and fell off the lorry, breaking an ankle. The unfortunate young idiot was put on a charge for causing a self-inflicted injury.

The scene on a platform at Darlington Railway Station, as the entire complement of the 14th Field Regiment, carrying their personal kit, boarded a 'special' for London, reminded me of those wartime propaganda films showing young heroes going off to war. The fact that some of the men in our regiment were kissing goodbye to girl friends, partly obscured by swirling smoke and steam from the engines, intensified thoughts of The Way Ahead and Millions Like Us. Anything to take my mind off my own loneliness!

I sat down in a crowded carriage. The air was already thick with cigarette smoke, some of it mine. The Clean Air Act had put paid to smog, but England was still a 'smoky' old country in 1959. I pondered on the dismal fact that I was running away again. I had given up my dream of becoming a journalist. I had left home, failing to give my mother the support she needed. I had left the Old Bell hotel because I hadn't been mature enough to handle an adult situation; now here I was, seemingly on the run again, by volunteering for service in Aden. You're doing well so far, Ward.

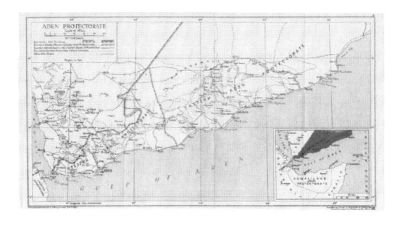

The Aden Protectorate

1839-1967

The British Protectorate evolved after various treaties were secured with the nine tribes inhabiting the 110,000 square miles {285000 sq km} of territory bordered by Yemen, Saudi Arabia and Oman. The strategic position of the port facilities were all-important to British interests.

2

Those Barren Rocks of Aden

'Lance Corporal Ward's a real-life soldier now.
Oh, Lance Corporal Ward's a real-life soldier now!
He can fire his gun in anger at the slightest sign of danger
Yes! Lance Corporal Ward's a real-life soldier now!'.

The Troopship Devonshire dropped anchor in Aden's great harbour.

An extinct volcano containing the aptly named town of Crater, rose up beyond the slightly more modern, Steamer Point, Decaying colonial-style buildings and dusty roads cringing beneath a blazing sun, were my first impressions of Steamer Point. The intense heat seemed to have slowed every one down to a snail's pace. Men dressed in white djellabahs and shemaghs lounged about under coffee shop awnings or mooched along in leather sandals as though they had all the time in the world. Plenty of daggers were on show in waistbands and most of the vehicles passing to and fro were in a sorry state.

The road to Khormaksar Airport and what was to be our base camp, Seedaseer Lines, followed the curve of the bay, with the notorious 'out of bounds' Maalla township on the right, until it came to a junction where the 'officers only' Shalimar night club stood in isolated splendour.

The Indian Ocean became visible on the far side of a broad stretch of sand on our right. This was unbelievable! Here I was, looking at the Indian Ocean while a camel train padded its way along the shore. A country boy's dreams can come true!

Seeing all this exotica from the back of an army lorry, I had an all too familiar sensation of being detached from reality; an observer, not a participator, watching the passing world as though it was nothing more than a newsreel. This odd approach to real life was possibly due to my fractured childhood.

Seedaserr Lines were surrounded on two sides by flat roofed, two-storied married quarters. They were more modern than the camp itself, which, in its layout and architectural style was reminiscent of Indian Army days.

Our billet inherited a pet monkey from its previous occupants. It was named Eccles, after an idiotic character in the 'Goon Show', the popular BBC radio comedy. The damn thing amused itself by stealing small items of kit and rushing off to sit on the roof, teasing us as we tried to persuade it to come down.

Within a few days of our arrival, a gun fitter fell asleep on the nearby beach and became so severely sunburned he was rushed to the nearby military hospital where he was packed in ice in order to save his life.

Then there was a bit of a punch-up in the NAAFI, over who knows what, after which, I followed a group of gunners to a disused building in the camp where a home-made porn film, involving a soldier's naked wife doing some extraordinary things with an army belt, was being surreptitiously shown. Youthful curiosity had to be satisfied.

Dhala, eighty, desert-track, miles from Aden, was hidden away in a high, verdant valley, a short distance from the troublesome border with Yemen. The area was full of dissident tribesmen busily working themselves up to a full-on Marxist revolution

I was soon on the way there with 1st Field battery RA. Our convoy consisted of four twenty-five pounders being towed by Bedfords, two Land Rovers, a Saladin armoured car, a signals vehicle, a water bowser and my ration lorry, known to one and all as the Q truck

.

After we had left the scruffy, dangerous townships of Zingibar and Sheikh Othman behind us and were on a desert track, I felt that I had come home. No metalled roads or fences in one hundred thousand square miles of undeveloped country. Great, barren vistas with a distant range of hills shimmering like mirages beneath a brazen sky. It was simply glorious! Here we are, dad; these wide open spaces may be exactly the opposite to being in 'the middle of a bloody great wood' but just as you always wanted, there aren't many regulators out here, and the only law is the law of survival!

We bounced along, half hidden by the clouds of dust we kicked up; my driver wrestling with the steering wheel. Apart from avoiding the worst of the terrain and maintaining convoy discipline, there were no rules of the road out here, either!

The 'Beau Geste' style, Fort Kutheir, hove in to view, but our 20th century vehicles shot past the nineteenth century and continued on their noisy, intrusive way. Their passengers weren't exactly tourists!

Fort Kutheir in 1959

Captain Evans brought the convoy to a halt on the approach to the menacing Khubeira, more commonly known as the Dhala, Pass. Blasted out of the mountainside by Royal Engineers, it climbed five thousand feet to a fertile escarpment. I produced a 'brew-up' and we all drank scalding-hot tea from our mess tins. This was a tricky little operation, because the heat of the tea was quickly transferred to the metal, creating blistered lips if one wasn't careful!

Several large hawks were circling in the sky above us, making me think of buzzards in Hollywood Westerns, indicating the position of cavalrymen killed by Indians, or vice-versa. These noble looking birds had a rather disdainful air about them but were quickly reduced to ignobility by being dubbed 'shite hawks' by the soldiers.

Inevitable gossip and rumour had spread amongst us. Snipers may be lurking on the heights surrounding the pass, waiting to take pot-shots at us.

Macho man put in an appearance.

'Them A-rabs can't shoot for toffee.'

'They've only got them banduks. They'd probably blow up in their faces if they used 'em.'

This was young, inexperienced men displaying bravado and telling jokes to cover up fear. Servicemen go forward because they are more afraid of what their comrades may think of them if they don't, than they are of what may happen to them when they do. All in the same boat.

Trained to use the .303 rifle, I'd done quite well with it on the firing range; swelling with pride when an officer remarked,

'That's good shooting, lance-corporal.'

I'd been re-trained when the SLR 7.62 replaced it, but I found the new weapon had some drawbacks for a left-hander like me. It certainly felt less comforting than the solid .303, and working the bolt was a little awkward for me.

Those rumours encouraged me to keep the weapon close at hand as my driver negotiated the twists and turns of the narrow pass. With a wall of rock rising hundreds of feet on the left and a plunging precipice on the right, those handling a heavily-laden three-tonner towing a one and a half ton 25 pounder, had a difficult, nerve-wracking job, especially on the sharp bends.

We arrived at the top without incident and drove in to what I considered to be the equivalent of James Hilton's, Shangri-La; a long and complex series of broad wadis, lost in mountains, five thousand feet above sea level, with scattered villages and children herding goats. We passed a camel train transporting qat to Aden. The dark green shrub was cultivated in small fields along the valleys. Many an Arab in the Protectorate was hooked on chewing their leaves. They were very stimulating; so much so that, back in Aden, the advice was, 'Never grab a ride in a taxi if its driver has green lips!'

The rocky crags, right on the Yemen border, were certainly within shooting distance as we continued on our way. Were they concealing dissident tribesmen engaged in trying to line us up in their sights? Captain Evans seemed to think so because he directed the convoy to where a group of thorn trees could partially conceal us. He posted guards while Privates Dagnan, and I produced a hot meal from the boxes of composite rations we carried. Each box contained sufficient canned food to last ten men for a day; breakfast, lunch and dinner. In addition most of them contained a tin of twenty cigarettes and ten bars of chocolate. Tinned bacon was considered to be the worst thing ever, and stewed steak the best.

What really impressed me about our two officers; I'm afraid I have forgotten the name of the young second lieutenant, was the fact that they always held back until their men had been fed before collecting their own share of whatever was on offer. The senior NCO, Sergeant Mathews, did likewise.

Mathews, aged about twenty eight, was the oldest among us. I doubt whether Captain Evans was more than twenty six, the second lieutenant being even younger. As for the rest of us, we were little more than teenagers. My nineteenth birthday was still three months away.

I couldn't help noticing that my 'travelling companions' had become noticeably calmer and more self-disciplined than they were when they were in barracks. Some of the training we had all received, seemed to have stuck.

Our camp, when we reached it, was a prepared site on rising ground with a distant view of a straggling village. To my mind it was rather too close for comfort to the craggy heights of a range of barren hills, providing plenty of convenient perches for snipers. Crude, dry stone walls had been built to create a defendable laager. In order to give warning of any infiltrators in the dead of night, they had been strung with a plethora of discarded metal objects, including empty composite ration tins.

Those ever present raptors circled high above the camp, waiting to swoop down and snatch food from the plate of an unsuspecting soldier crossing from the field kitchen to a marquee that had been erected for communal purposes.

We were ordered to beat the outers of our two-man tents every morning because enormous camel spiders liked to climb in to them for extra warmth during the night. The size of dinner plates, they were both hairy and scary! We had to keep our eyes open for scorpions, as well.

Those below the rank of sergeant were left uninformed about the how and why of things. We all had our individual jobs to do, so we just got on with them without asking silly questions like, 'Why are we here, sir?'

Foot patrols were organized. I can only suppose they were undertaken in order to make the British Army's presence felt in the area. Always ready for a diversion, I inveigled myself on to them whenever I could get away with it.

Clutching our weapons, we tramped the length and breadth of the hills and valleys. It was fascinating to see stick insects, chameleons and beautifully coloured small birds living among the foliage of the acacia trees and what I now believe to be the common myrrh.

An unfortunate kid, heading for the cooking pot
They make a yummy curry!

Being on foot patrol became even more interesting when we marched boldly down the unpaved, rubble-strewn street of a sloping village. While charming, bare foot children ran excitedly alongside us, the adult male inhabitants watched in a sullen silence that made me feel distinctly uneasy. They were armed to the teeth, as usual. What few women we 'saw' were actually completely hidden from view in their black as black can be, burqas; turning their backs on us as we passed by. Somewhere beneath those all-encompassing garments were human beings with the same thoughts and feelings as the rest of the human race. Were they happy about their sex being so enslaved for so many centuries?

gh what almost amounted to jungle during one of these patrols, a sudden deluge brought down myriads of small fish with it. Sucked up, somewhere out in the Indian Ocean, they had been carried helplessly on the wind, to be dropped on the mountains along with the rain.

As they wriggled on the ground in countless numbers, I contemplated collecting some of them and frying them for the lads when we returned to camp. Those who were with me didn't think much of the idea, so, unavoidably trampling them beneath our feet, we continued on our way.

The shooting began in the middle of the night, scarifying me out of my sleeping bag and sending me fumbling for my SLR in the darkness of my tent.

A few rounds of rifle fire, aimed at us from somewhere on the nearby hills, produced a massive response. Tracer shells arced across the sky as the Browning on the Saladin opened up. A section of 1st Field Battery's gunners were ordered to return fire with their rifles. They stood, or crouched by the perimeter wall, using the semi-automatic system on their SLR's until being ordered to cease fire. On this occasion I could only stand and watch. I was merely an 'extra' who wasn't required on set for that particular scene.

Silence fell; the moon still shone brightly, illuminating an enormous canopy of stars; and we were all still alive. Whether any dissidents had been killed or wounded was impossible to tell.

An RAF Pembroke aircraft flew rations and mail in from Khormaksar. Making a landing on the tricky Dhala airstrip was never easy. A couple of aircraft had been written off in the past; but those young pilots made light work of it-most of the time.

I returned from the airstrip with supplies one morning to discover that Private Dagnan had virtually destroyed the field kitchen. The rule was: 'never fiddle with a petrol burner in the close vicinity of one that has already been lit'.

With two burners facing each other in a long trench, Dagnan had difficulty lighting the second of them. He had continued trying until flames from the first one reached the fine spray of petrol emerging from the second. They had both exploded.

Badly singed and almost hairless, Dagnan survived the blast, but most of our rations were destroyed; the tins swollen and blackened by the flames and tremendous heat that had been created.

Captain Evans was obliged to send a signal to Aden requesting two new burners. In the meantime, we managed to borrow one from a squadron of Aden Protectorate Levies camped further down the valley.

My friend, Mick Beaney, received some letters and a couple of out-of-date county newspapers. They brought me the girl who was to change my life. She appeared in the form of a photograph in one of the newspaper that Mick tossed in my direction after he'd finished with it. Daphne stood out among a group of girls involved in youth club activities. Her pretty face had a no-nonsense look about it, showing that she was deeply unimpressed by having her name in the papers. Lonely as hell, I made up my mind to write an open letter to her. I did so in carefully couched terms, sending it to her via the newspaper, as I had no idea where she lived.

A few weeks later I received a reply. Daphne's mother had cajoled her in to writing to 'that poor boy out there in the desert!' A long period of correspondence had begun

3

The Jinxed Patrol

I cannot recall our twenty-five pounders being fired in anger while we were in Dhala, but there had been a sufficient exchange of small arms fire to keep us amused until we returned to our base at Seedaseer Lines.

With no opportunity for me to work in an officers' mess, I brewed and stewed in the camp's main kitchen. Never mind, with Tusker beer costing next to nothing in the NAAFI and two hundred cigarettes for seven and sixpence (37p at today's value) life wasn't too bad. What's more, a vast strip of sandy beach and the warm Indian Ocean was within five minutes walk of my billet. Most of us common soldiery preferred using the open-air swimming pool on that beach, because that's where the nubile nurses and daughters of servicemen were obliged to gather in their itsy-bitsy bikinis. Displaying so much female flesh on the beach itself was absolutely forbidden, or haraam, as the Arabs would say. We circled those girls and homed in on them like bees heading for a pot of honey, mostly without success. Nurses saved themselves for officers, and hairy sergeants saved their daughters from predators like us.

1st Field Battery was soon off again; this time we had what seemed to us lesser mortals, to be a roving commission in the north-eastern part of the Aden Protectorate. Not much in the way of high country here, only distant escarpments, scrubland and endless desert as we headed in the direction of the Empty Quarter.

We camped in the heat of the day near some squalid, empty

huts that had once passed for a village. I set up a temporary kitchen inside one of them.

While I was leaning against an outside wall, drenched in sweat as a result of the unusually high humidity and smoking the inevitable cigarette, the lowering sun became obscured. Then the westerly horizon disappeared behind an immense wall of sand. Driven by a powerful wind, it was heading straight for us!

Everyone took cover. The Saladin and Ferret armoured car crews climbed inside their vehicles and closed the hatches as the gunners either climbed aboard or slid beneath the lorries. I dropped my cigarette, shot in to my temporary kitchen, and shut the door.

The sand storm hit us with tremendous force After the door to my shelter was blown in by the sheer pressure it produced, I found myself blinded and choking on sand. Away went the roof! I battled my way outside and feeling that I was in danger of literally being blown away myself, strove to get to a sheltering lorry. Before I could do so, the storm was gone. Like a strange and uncontrollable living thing, it rampaged across the desert, pursued by swirling dust devils until it died a natural death somewhere in the distant hills.

Three dozen men were left covered from head to foot in dust, my No 1 burners were buried. The dixies and ration boxes, barely visible, were tumbled in an untidy heap against a wall, and every metal object in the convoy was crackling with static electricity; we discovered that little fact straight away!

The sun came out again and we began the clean-up operation.

This was the first of several incidents that convinced one or two of the morbid among us that the patrol was jinxed.

Led by two good officers and a decent sergeant, we were the usual motley band of soldiers. Captain Evans, although not very tall, had an air of quiet authority about him. He was respected for his light touch when it came to issuing orders, as was our second lieutenant. Three good men who, as I saw it, only let us down in one respect. They never told us what was happening from one day to the next. Only they knew what our aims were and why we were heading off in to the wild, blue yonder. I could, perhaps, have asked them, but it wasn't the done thing at the time.

Sergeant Mathews was gingery in both his hair and his treatment of those who let the side down. Our gun fitter was a tough guy- a fighter when drunk. It had taken all those on duty in the guard room to restrain him one night in Seedaseer Lines. This was after he had broken the noses of two MP's. His drunken rages were awesome to behold and his punishments light because his skills were needed to keep the battery of guns in good order.

Jim Felton, a cunning old sweat who knew the ropes, had taught me some of the local 'lingo' during the voyage out. How to say please, thank you and ask the price of something, etcetera; Yes indeed! Jim passed on every Arabic swear word and deadly insult he knew!

Bombardier Whiteside was a stocky Irishman. He had been a drinking partner of mine back in Darlington. None of us in 1st

Field Battery were aware that the worm of insanity was eating away at his mind.

We'd been ordered to bring only a limited amount of personal items with us on this patrol; the less weight we carried, the better chance we had of successfully making our way across what proved to be some of the most difficult terrain on earth for heavy guns and vehicles.

Whiteside had wanted to bring some long playing records and a gramophone; either wind-up or battery powered, I don't know which, that he had purchased in Steamer Point. The fact that Captain Evans had refused to allow him to do so was now festering away in his disturbed mind.

Boy! How nice it would have been to have taken a shower after that sand storm, but we could only dream of having one. That little luxury was back at base camp, about seventy miles away.

Our water supply was carried in the tank of a sturdy bowser lorry. It was carefully rationed. After a few days, the only way to make the stuff drinkable was to stir copious amounts of lemonade powder in to it, or brew up some tea with plenty of sweet Fussels milk added.

The ration truck broke down on a desolate gravel plain where only thorn bush had managed to take root. It was hot-hot-hot, I kid you not!

Captain Evans must have been trying to keep to some sort of schedule he preferred not to talk about, because after ensuring we had sufficient water to last a couple of days, he ordered the rest of the convoy to continue; leaving us with a REME corporal who knew what the problem was, and a Ferret armoured car with its two man crew, for protection.

The five of us watched the convoy until it was finally out of sight. Did I mention it was hot?

The REME guy was obliged to use his beret as a kind of oven glove when it came to opening the lorry's bonnet.

We all swallowed some salt tablets. The vastness of the surroundings in which we appeared to be the only living things, had us talking almost in whispers. We were temporarily stranded in a world where silence usually reigned. Now it was being broken, rather eerily, by the noise made by whatever tool our mechanic was using.

The soldiers manning the Ferret belonged to a squadron of what I'm fairly certain were the 17/21st Lancers. Cigarettes were passed round-and round again, then the ration truck's engine burst in to life. Well done, that man.

Now all we had to do was catch up with the rest of the convoy, or make our way to the map reference Captain Evans had provided us with.

We set out across the plain, leaving it to the boys in the Ferret just ahead of us, to contact the convoy on their radio.

The Ferret stopped, so we stopped. Their radio was malfunctioning.

The REME corporal thought he knew why.

'It's because of the miles of rocks and such-like, lying around. They're full of iron, or something that buggers up the radios.'

We continued on our sweating, swearing way. The landscape remained devoid of any life, both flora and fauna, until we left the rock and gravel plain behind us and found ourselves back in sandy scrubland.

The Ferret stopped; we stopped. One of the lancers waved at us and shouted,

'Got 'em. They ain't far off!'

Out of touch with the convoy

We found 1st Field Battery laagered and waiting for me to cook their dinner for them.

This site, on the edge of country similar to the badlands of the Old West, as seen in many a John Ford movie, became our home for a while. A latrine was dug within its perimeter where three soldiers could sit side by side, have a conversation and share a three weeks old newspaper.

Our twenty-five pounders pointed directly down a broad valley that ran through a tangle of ochre-coloured hills. There was a large village somewhere down there. According to gossip it was full of dissident tribesmen. If a group isn't kept informed by those in charge of them, the rumours spread, causing alarm and despondency. I learnt that lesson. It came in handy when I grew up and found myself in charge of people.

It was decent of the local inhabitants to wait until we got settled in before they began firing at us.

'STAND TO!'

We did so; in the dark in more ways than one. In response to some 'incoming', an over excited member of the Saladin's crew opened up with the vehicle's Browning machine gun. His enthusiasm was better than his aim, because he managed to shred the screen that surrounded our primitive toilet facility. Fortunately for him, no one was using it at the time. There were no visible targets for any of us to shoot at, apart from a distant muzzle flare, but the rest of us returned fire as ordered, using our SLRs. We created more than enough explosive noises to rip apart the silence that passeth mans' understanding; the desert at night.

Anti climax. And so to bed, or back to it, anyway.

Come morning, and the Intelligence boys must have been at work, because our second lieutenant and a Royal Signals corporal set off for the hills in order to establish an observation post from which they would be able to direct artillery fire. It sounded like a very risky task, but I knew nothing about such undertakings.

Range details and corrections for the fall of shot were relayed by radio from the OP to the signals vehicle standing behind the guns. From there they were shouted out to the gun crews.

'Up one hundred!'

Swift work by the teams, then…

'Fire!'

'Left one hundred!'

Make adjustments. Repeat the loading process.

'Fire!'

Four guns banged and flashed in unison, sending high explosive shells to land on targets over half a mile away.

The 'jinx' was still with us because there was a rare misfire. A shell remained in the breech of one of the guns. It was a dangerous moment. All firing stopped and the gun crews stepped away from their positions. It was Sergeant Mathews' job to clear that breech; never mind the fact that the shell might explode at any moment. Treating the whole thing as purely routine, he removed both the cartridge and the shell, and we all breathed again.

When the entire battery moved up to the village, it became apparent that we hadn't been shelling it after all; the fire had been directed elsewhere.

Here was yet another poverty-stricken community, living on a barren slope in simple houses built of local stone, of which there was plenty! The children were delightful, the men sinister and the females, dressed as they were, could have been from another planet as far as we were concerned.

Before we returned to our camp, our medic patched up the face of one of the children who had suffered some kind of accident. The purpose of our little visit was revealed. We were there to pick up the headmen, offer them our hospitality and show them what our 25 pounders could do.

Only rumours again, but the word went round that the villagers were not paying their tithes to the sheikh who controlled the area. We were giving him a helping hand in persuading them to do so. It was all conjecture, but that's what you get when you are not 'kept in the loop', as they say today.

The gunners, with accurate fire and maximum elevation, duly knocked the top off the nearest mountain and the suitably impressed headmen were taken back home by Captain Evans himself.

The OP needed supplies and it fell to me to deliver them. Their position was just about accessible by Land Rover if one took a circuitous route to it. I wondered about such things as 'revealing their position to the enemy' but whatever importance was placed on that was outweighed by the fact that the operation, whatever it was, was taking longer than had been expected. Those manning the OP were running short of food and water.

As it turned out, I never did get to see the OP myself. My driver, a Manchester lad, managed to get our Land Rover so severely bogged down, no amount of sand mats or digging would extricate us.

The nervous driver didn't want to be left alone and he didn't want to hack it all the way back to camp on his own. I wasn't prepared to pull rank on him, but I wasn't prepared to leave our vehicle unguarded, either. Having a radio with us would have helped. That was my fault. Inexperienced, I had treated this little trip like an excursion and a diversion. I didn't exactly have a 'military' mind.

Idiotically, we sat side by side in the heat of the day, in a Land Rover that was up to its axles in sand. The usual inner debate took place. 'Shall I go back to base and get help? Should I make the driver go? Should we both go? For goodness sake, you're in charge, so make a decision, Ward!

Oh, oh; three Arabs appeared out of nowhere and squatted down, fifty yards away. They were staring intently at us. I gripped the butt of the Stirling I had brought with me. I had only fired one of the things during training, which at that moment, felt to be a lifetime ago. The driver and I had already been sweating, now we began swearing as well; rather quietly, because we didn't want to upset the neighbors.

Now there were six or seven Arabs watching us. They were armed to the teeth with long barrelled rifles, bandoliers full of ammo and great, curved daggers at their waists. Bloody hell!

This was the point where I revealed to my driver, whatever his name was, that I had not only seen too many movies, I thought I was taking part in one. I wasn't an 'extra', either; this time I had a starring role!

After making a fine display of putting my Stirling to one side, I stepped out of the Land Rover and, with arms outstretched, crossed the burning hot sand to where the Arabs were taking their ease. That part of my psychological make-up, which somehow managed to keep me feeling detached from reality, allowed me to be nonchalance personified.

By the time this little event took place I had picked up a bit more of the language than Felton had taught me, so I was able to greet them and ask them how they were, without uttering deadly insults.

Big grins showed through the Arabs beards, and there they were, shaking my hand and welcoming me as though I was a long-lost relative.

I sat down with them, crossing my legs and trying my hardest to observe the niceties by not pointing my feet at any of them. One of the Arabs took a chapatti from a bag, tore a piece from it and gave it to me. I quite liked chapattis.

They declined my offer of the warm lemonade I had in my water bottle, so I handed round some cigarettes. I had taken to smoking Peter Stuyvesant. They seemed to like them; cupping their hands round them and inhaling the smoke through their fingers. Friendly as they were, the Arabs ignored my attempts to persuade the whole lot of them to get off their backsides and push the Land Rover out of the hole it had dug for itself. Manual labour for a Bedu? No chance. It was beneath their dignity.

One of the Arabs made a decision, scrambled to his feet, and after exchanging a few words with the others, set off in the direction of our camp. Having noticed that I hadn't had my throat cut, my driver strolled across to join me, and an hour or so later, a Bedford three-tonner, complete with winch, hove in to view and soon dragged us out of our embarrassing situation.

Before that lorry arrived the Arabs had said their farewells and strolled away as though they were embarking on a country walk.

I have no idea what became of the Arab who went all that distance to the camp in order to get help. I would have liked to have thanked him, but I never saw him again.

Sergeant Mathews thought he'd better deliver those rations to the OP. We couldn't be trusted with a bleeding Matchbox toy, let alone a man-sized army vehicle.

Whether that particular area was far less dangerous than we, who weren't in the know, imagined it was, or whether the Arabs in question had been observing some ancient rule of desert hospitality, was a hotly debated subject when we returned to camp.

1st Field Battery's next move took us about thirty miles beyond the remote desert township of Ataq.

This time, we took up residence in a fortified house that had a walled compound large enough for us to park all our vehicles in, leaving room for me to set up a field kitchen.

Guards were posted on the roof of the keep-like, three-storied house, which provided a 360 degree view of both the desert stretching away towards Ataq and the nearby rugged hill country, through which rebel factions could make easy passage after crossing the ill-defined Yemen border.

Morale was naturally a bit low among us lesser mortals; no wine, women or song and very little prospect of having access to any of them for the foreseeable future. To try and combat this, Sergeant Mathews organised an alcohol-free party in the dirt-floored main room of the keep. I prepared what I could in the way of party food and the officers joined in when Mathews encouraged each of us in turn to tell our favourite jokes and sing songs of our own choosing. He really jollied us along. Pathetically, the only song I could think of was, 'The Lincolnshire Poacher', remembered from my school days. Fortunately for me, unlike Tom, when he sings it in Tom Brown's Schooldays, there was no Flashman present to throw things at me. Sergeant Mathews managed an amusing song that was based on army call signs.

A Blackburn Beverley at hot and dusty Ataq

The following day happened to be Whit Sunday. Towards evening, after cleaning my rifle and suspending it from the roof of my tent to keep it so, I emerged and began to cross the compound. Paddy Whiteside was walking towards me, on his way to mount guard. Captain Evans came out of the door that led to the room where we had held our little party the night before. All three of us converged on one another. The usual exchange of pleasantries took place as our paths crossed. ithout any warning whatsoever, Whiteside lifted the muzzle of his Stirling and shot Captain Evans at point blank range. Emitting no more than what sounded to me like a sigh, the officer fell to the ground. I froze, of course. Whiteside turned towards me. There were no wildly staring eyes, no demented grin, no screams, just a blank expression on his face as he pointed the muzzle of his gun in my direction. I unfroze as my brain went in to survival mode. Off I went in a short, swerving run towards a stone shed that was built in to the perimeter wall. I was currently using it as a ration store. Just before I reached it, Whiteside, who must have either fumbled with the Stirling or hesitated for a moment, fired a short burst. Bullets whanged against the shed's craggy wall as I crashed headlong through its doorway. This was something more than pointing a rifle over a parapet and firing in the general direction of an unseen enemy. I wasn't imagining that I was acting in a B movie now. This was the real me, involved in a real life and death drama.

Then the shouting started; coming from various parts of the fort. Gunners wanted to know what the hell was happening.

Whiteside was yelling at the top of his voice, as well; warning everyone to stay away from him, and calling for Sergeant Mathews at the same time. I have no recollection of the actual words Whiteside used; all I know is, they were enough to make everyone keep their heads down, wherever they happened to be.

A long distance shouting match ensued between the sergeant and the deranged bombardier. Mathews did everything he could to try and persuade Whiteside to put his weapon down. He wasn't having it, though. Every now and again, in the increasing darkness, he fired a few random shots, while I, with my eyes adjusted to the gloom in my hiding place, was thinking wild thoughts. 'He had been just out of reach, but I wonder if I should have made an attempt to get that gun away from him, instead of diving in here? He had four or five seconds in which to shoot me; then when he tried to, he missed. Had he hesitated because we'd got drunk together a couple of times? No, that couldn't have been the reason, because it would indicate lucid thinking on his part If he comes through that door, I'll bash him with this spade!' and so on.

I had discovered the spade leaning against a wall. It was the one we used to dig rubbish pits beyond the perimeter walls.

Then came the unmistakable sound of a rifle shot. Whiteside cried out in agony. I looked cautiously out of the door. In the gathering darkness I could see that he was writhing about on the ground, a scant few yards away.

I hurried over to him.

'Hail Mary, mother of God!' The bombardier was repeating the phrase over and over again. Believing him to be dying, I sat down next to him.

Controlling the desire to reach out and place a comforting hand on Captain Evan's still form, and surrounded by those who had arrived seconds after me, I placed Whiteside's head in my lap and began reciting the Lord's Prayer.

The second lieutenant examined our battery commander's body while Sergeant Mathews injected Whiteside with ampoules of morphine. He had been shot in the thigh. Those who knew how to do such things took care of the wound, using large field dressings.

The smallest man in 1st Field Battery, Gunner Lusher, had wounded Whiteside. Using his own initiative, he had made his way to the castellated, flat roof of the house. Once there, he had felled the bombardier's shadowy figure with a single shot.

The second lieutenant had our good captain's body covered properly and placed in the back of a one-tonner, so close to the man who'd murdered him, they were touching. It was necessary to take them to the Aden Protectorate levies camp at Ataq- immediately.

I don't know why I was ordered to accompany the driver. Perhaps it was because I'd been first on the scene and had said a prayer for Captain Evans and Whiteside; something as simple as that. It just happened that way.

'I will signal Ataq to let them know you are on your way, lance corporal. Drive carefully and watch out for hidden wadis.'

'Yes, sir, I will.'

I wasn't actually doing the driving, so I passed those instructions on to the gunner who was.

With the one-tanner's headlights showing us the way, we set off across the virtually trackless desert towards Ataq and its airstrip. The driver and I, well aware of our grim cargo, chain smoked and tried to deal with the tragic event as best we could.

'What the-?'

We both saw them at the same time. A multitude of headlights were heading towards us, line abreast.

CRASH ACTION!

Used in a dire emergency, guns, vehicles, the whole damned thing, cross any form of negotiable country, going flat out, only deviating from their course if it is necessary to avoid insurmountable objects, until they reach their objective.

That was exactly what a squadron of APL was doing.

They homed in on our one-tonner, surrounding us in a blaze of headlights, masked with the dust their vehicles had created.

A British officer came and spoke to us. It quickly emerged that the signal sent by our second lieutenant had been misinterpreted by whoever had received it, leaving the APL with the impression that our camp was under attack, our battery commander had been killed and a bombardier seriously wounded.

The squadron had been coming flat out to our rescue.

After the unconscious Whiteside and Captain Evan's body had been transferred to one of their vehicles, the driver and I returned to the fortified house.

Late the following day, two members of the Special Investigations Branch arrived. They had flown from Aden to Ataq in double-quick time, then escorted to our camp.

We all made statements about where we were and what we did before, during and after the shooting. Both investigators found it hard to accept my testimony that Whiteside 'just did it', and, no, there hadn't been any heated exchanges between the bombardier and the captain before he was shot. When I suggested it may have happened because they'd had an argument about a record player before we left Seedaseer Lines, the SIB men gave me a pitying look.

Something else has always slightly concerned me about the Whiteside incident. When I reached him after he'd been shot, I noticed that he had armed himself with Captain Evans' service revolver. He had been thinking clearly enough to remove it from the officer's holster. I never drew attention to that and as far as I know, it was never mentioned elsewhere.

Those who knew best, thought it essential that 1st Field Battery continued with its patrol. We did so, entering the roughest country we had yet encountered. Our 25 pounders had to be winched every foot of the way. Those Bedfords were tough, all right; moving a winch-cable's length over impossible terrain, winching the guns forward, then moving up to repeat the process all day long. Did I mention it was blisteringly hot?

In that manner, we managed about one mile per hour. The British Army was, apparently, determined to show those invisible rebels that we could get at them wherever they went.

Thankfully, we came to the end of that sort of country after a couple of days. We were on the desert floor again, heading for what passed for home; Seedaseer Lines.

A 'jinx' was still haunting the patrol. Our young second lieutenant made a mistake. He ordered us to stop for the night in the bed of a wadi.

It was the usual routine for Dagnan and me. Set up the kitchen, feed the lads, make ready for the morning, then crawl into our tent and hope to sleep, undisturbed.

Sergeant Mathew's bladder saved us from a serious soaking and possible death. As dawn was breaking, he took a stroll along the wadi in order to find a secluded spot he could use as a toilet. He turned a bend- and forgot all about doing so. A four feet high wall of water was rushing towards him, pushing all sorts of debris in front of it. I suppose he froze and unfroze, just as I had when Whiteside shot Captain Evans, then came charging back down the wadi to where we were camped, shouting and waving his arms about. Emerging from our tents and rubbing sleep from our eyes, we saw at once the thing that had excited our sergeant so much. It was 'Bloody hell!' time again! My, how we scrambled up the sides of that wadi! Mathews, having woken us up from our beauty sleep, followed our example.

The flash flood rushed by, taking a Land Rover and one or two of our tents with it. Even the three-tonners and moured vehicles were slewed out of position by the force of the water.

'There must have been quite a rainstorm up in those mountains last night.' That would have been said by one of us, wouldn't it?

Most of our kit was intact because, it being only a night stop, we hadn't bothered unloading the Bedfords.

We can laugh about it now the flood has subsided.

After our REME mechanic made the Land Rover live again, we continued on our way; fetching up at Seedaseer Lines two or three days later.

The first thing one of our number did, when we got there, was to infiltrate Khormaksar Airport in the middle of the night and attempt to smuggle himself on board an RAF Transport Command 'plane, bound for the UK. He was caught by the RAF police and after due process, was cas-evaced home. He got what he wanted, but had to do it through the system, see?

I was due to go on leave to Mombasa. Like everyone else in 1st Field Battery, I needed some serious R and R. It was not to be, however; not for yours truly, it wasn't. Bombardier Whiteside had recovered sufficiently from his wound to stand trial for murder. On the very day my leave started, I was ordered to attend his court martial as a witness.

That did it for me! Having built up a considerable amount of money to blow in Mombasa, I decided to spend the whole lot on one mad night out in Aden. I invited several members of my billet to come with me. I was buying!

The invitation was, in part, an attempt to tie myself more closely to the soldiers I served with. Not to put too fine a point on it, my Ernest Hemingway failed to blend with their Hank Janson. The personality I'd been born with, rubbed theirs up the wrong way.

Thoughts of Ezra **Pound's, 'In Durance'

'I am homesick after mine own kind,
Oh, I know that there are folk about me,
Friendly faces,
But I am homesick after mine own kind.'.

I never realised it at the time, but there must have been others in the group who felt the same as me; they just made a better job of hiding their true feelings than I did. I could not always, 'Sit in the corner of the carriage, scribbling stories.' as I'd done in my boyhood days. Sometimes it was necessary for me to break out of my shell and let rip. This was one of those occasions.

In Steamer Point's 'Rock' Hotel, the more I drunk, the more I insisted on paying for everything and everybody. That suited my hangers-on very well.

An orgiastic night of folly ensued. We left Steamer Point at an ungodly hour, intent on 'raiding' Maalla. We were looking for the infamous 'Maalla Mary' and the home-made hooch it was rumoured the Arabs brewed up in the brothels, 'using dates, and stuff.' We took a noisy, belligerent step too far.

As we staggered noisily along an unpaved road lined with hovels, Arab men began to follow us; emerging from dark alleyways and side roads until there were quite a few of them. They weren't at all happy with our presence.

The pace picked up. They were closing in on us! It is surprising how fast even drunk men can run when they are being pursued by a small mob of anti-British Arabs, armed with big, curved daggers. So this was why Maalla was out of bounds!

We made it to the beach, split up and lost them somewhere near the military hospital, or perhaps they just gave up chasing us.

What fools we mortals be! I was broke-again, and a few days later I was also 'all broke-up' when I was informed that I would not be required to give evidence at Whiteside's court martial. A plea of guilty but insane had been lodged and accepted.

I'd missed the opportunity to have a jolly jaunt to Mombasa and Whiteside had been sentenced to be detained in a military asylum for an indeterminate period. As far as I was concerned,

Captain Evans death was somehow made even more of a tragedy when I discovered that his father was a clergyman.

In August, 1st Field Battery was due to take ship to Hong Kong, where it would rejoin the rest of 14th Field Regiment RA.

I was doing my duty by reading Daily Routine Orders on the

battery office notice board. A Foreign Office recruiting poster was pinned to it, advertising the fact that the Trucial Oman Scouts required a junior NCO chef with field experience.

I'd heard plenty of stories about this elite force since I'd been in Aden. It was said they were a cross between the Long Range Desert Group, the SAS and the French Foreign Legion; and what's more they didn't give a bugger about anything or anybody.

Without mentioning it to anyone I put my name down for the job; but company clerks were notoriously loose-mouthed, so word got out.

'What sort of weirdo prefers to go a thousand miles up the arse hole of the world, where he'll probably end up getting shot by some A-rab, when he could be spending a couple of years in a cushy posting like Hong Kong? I always knew that Ward bloke wasn't right in the head.'

I didn't stand a chance of being accepted by the Trucial Oman Scouts, but I was that weirdo, all right, and I probably wasn't right in the head. I liked the desert!

4

Interlude in Hong Kong

Before we set out for that 'dream posting' I want to mention Linda Yeung, a pretty little Chinese Christian I was to have a harmless friendship with. Wherever she is now, I do hope she can forgive me for using her name for the treacherous femme fatale in my novel, 'The Levelling Dust'.

It was either the troopship Nevasa or Oxfordshire that brought me and many another soldier from Aden to Hong Kong at the beginning of August 1960. The one that it wasn't, was to carry me back there in December! I feel obliged to put it like that because if I write that it was definitely the Nevasa, or definitely the Oxfordshrie, that carried me in one direction or the other, as sure as eggs are eggs, some character I haven't seen or heard from for fifty years, will pop up and say,

'Oh, no it wasn't!'

Damn know-all.

I enjoyed another two weeks' cruise at the taxpayers' expense. We crossed the Indian Ocean in glorious weather, just like the travel brochure promised.

In a typical Cinemascope, David Lean-style incident, our outward bound troopship encountered one on its way home. Hundreds of soldiers lined the rails on both vessels whistling, cheering, jeering and waving, all on the deep blue sea under a bright blue sky, as we passed one another. The thoughts of us outward-bound types turned inevitably to home.

I was unable to go ashore at Colombo. Someone in authority

spotted that I hadn't done a stroke of work for a week and promptly put me in charge of the fire piquet while we were at anchor there.

In Penang, the military police had their work cut out dealing with a multitude of soldiers seeking to break a selection of the seven deadly sins. In back street bars, pathetic, expressionless girls were literally lined up by their pimps; allowing their potential customers to take their pick. Pitiful. I witnessed it but didn't partake.

'Three days pay stopped.' Major Bowen imposed the same punishment on all those brought before him on the morning after the night before. The army saved itself a fair bit of money that day.

As the troopship sailed through the tail end of a typhoon, some of us gleefully risked our necks by using the tilting decks as slides. Being immortal, we survived our own stupidity and reached the 'Beautiful Harbour'- Hong Kong.

1st Field Battery, re-united with the regiment, was once again helping to guard a border.

We were based in a camp at Sek Kong Airfield in the New Territories. It was close to the overwhelming numerical might of Communist China.

Green hills and warm rain; paved roads, bus services and cafes in nearby Kam Tin were all in remarkable contrast to the deserts of the Aden Protectorate. My work wasn't onerous, but the daily routines a soldier in barracks follows, if he knows what's good for him, were very boring. Being in charge of the cooks' billet, I had my own quarters and a Chinese boy to take care of my kit. No, I wasn't a colonial slave owner. That boy, a bit of an entrepreneur who's probably a millionaire by now, got paid a little bit more than he asked for.

The most difficult task I had was that of trying to get the men to take their daily Paludrine tablet. Half of them seemed convinced that I was actually dosing them up with a bromide rather than giving them some protection against malaria.

****

'Why you long face?'

I was sitting in the Sweet Garden restaurant in Kam Tin one evening, when a young waitress asked me the question. Just as biting into a Madeleine did for Proust, it provided me with an instant memory of things past. In my case, it took me back to Bexhill Technical School and my English master, Mr. Barnes, who, when I put in an appearance, was apt to say,

'Here's Ward, looking jaundiced, as usual.'

After reassuring the girl that I wasn't particularly unhappy, I asked her name.

'It is Linda Yeung,' she smiled- and smiled again when she brought me the Tiger beer I'd ordered.

Apart from exchanging a few kisses, a purely platonic friendship ensued, with Linda's fiercely protective mother lurking constantly in the background; fearful that I might whisk her daughter off to England as my wife. Many a British soldier had married local girls before I came along, and no doubt, continued to do so after I left.

Personally, I had already formed a sense of loyalty to Daphne, the girl I was still writing to, but had yet to meet; so Linda's mother had nothing to fear on that score. It was however, rather nice to have a girl holding my hand as we went for walks in the local countryside. Rather annoyingly, Linda always managed to bring one or two other smiling, toothy, waitresses along with her, as chaperones.

Sometimes, having been invited to tea by two friends of mine; an artillery sergeant and his wife, we would climb a steep, narrow lane, through a jungle of tropical trees and plants, to their isolated bungalow on top of the hill. This pleasant, off-duty pastime ceased after the sergeant asked me to come to the bungalow alone one particular evening. I duly went along.

Half way through a meal that had been cooked by a Chinese servant girl, known as an Ayah or Amah, the sergeant glanced at his wife, Mary, who was sitting at the opposite end of the table to me, then said,

'You can have Mary, tonight, if you want to, Terry. I'm sleeping with the Amah.'

The compliant, curvy, Mary, smiled sweetly at me, letting me know that it was all right with her.

I politely declined their kind offer; thanked them in apologetic tones and said to Mary that I hoped she wasn't offended.

I left their bungalow a little earlier than I'd intended to.

Sad to say, several days passed before I was able to stop thinking carnal thoughts about the voluptuous Mary.

Not all army married quarters were hot beds of vice and sexual shenanigans, of course, but events such as the one I've just described, and the 'mucky' film I'd seen in Aden; added to the stories that circulated, helped me decide that I would never ask a wife of mine to live in such places; if I ever had a wife, that was!

My Hong Kong posting was short, but sweet indeed. Diving into the frenetic nightlife in Kowloon and on Victoria Island, made a welcome change to that of the rural New Territories, with its duck ponds, peaceful scenery and ancient villages. Paid on Friday, broke by Monday.

In early December 1960, I was sent for by the Battery Clerk. He informed me that I'd been accepted by the Trucial Oman Scouts. A place would be arranged for me on a troopship bound for the UK the following week. It would drop me off at Aden; if I still wanted to join the elite force.

In movie terms, think 'Wizard of Oz'. Its story begins in black and white, indicating dull, real life. It then transforms itself in to full blown colour when a tornado takes Dorothy to fantasy land.

My own journey wasn't to Oz, but to the equally fantastical land of the Seven Sheikhdoms. I travelled there at a speed rather slower than that of a tornado; movingat the rate of about twelve knots for most of the way.

I had always felt that I was something of a square peg in 14th Field Regiment. Although I understood the necessity for it, I disliked too much regimentation. I was fortunate to serve in a corps that escaped the worst of it, doing things by numbers was anathema to me.

When I finally arrived at the TOS camp on the fringe of Sharjah; I soon realised that I had at last, 'Found a ho-o-o-me in the army!' as a soldier in the film 'Battleground' repeats several times during its depiction of the Battle of the Bulge.

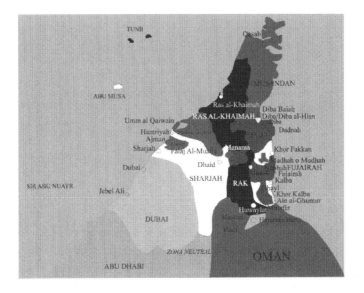

The seven sheikhdoms in which the Trucial Oman Scouts maintained law and order were: Abu Dhabi, Dubai, Sharjah, Ras al Khaimah, Ajman, Fujairah and Umm al Qaiwain; a total area of about 33, 000 sq miles; 83,000 sq km to the converted!

The Sheikh of Sharjah's Palace c1960

5

The Trucial Oman Scouts

A good deal of this chapter also appears in
'ARE YOU THE MAN?'
See the TOS Website

A typical desert well in the Seven Sheikhdoms

A nineteen, going on twenty years old lance-corporal, I stood at
the rail of the Oxfordshire/ Nevasa, I honestly can't remember
which, crammed between others of my ilk. I was looking down
at Linda Yeung and another attractive young waitress from the
Sweet Garden Restaurant as they waved a tearful goodbye to me
from where they stood on the crowded Kowloon Dock.

Before I had boarded the ship, Linda had revealed to me that it
was her ambition to marry a British soldier, preferably me, and
be whisked away to that wonderland, the western world. Sorry
to disappoint you, Lin; it can't be me. Sometime later, I
scribbled the following in a note book. Cruelty was not my

intention.

Chinee Girl

Lin Yeung she is Hong Kong girl,
She speekee pidgin Engleesh
Her mama 'fraid I marree Lin,
For she is young and singleesh
But mama has no need to fear,
Though daughter is good lookee,
Me no marree Chinee girl
'Cos I no like their cookee!

I was never a lover of Chinese food.

Multi-coloured streamers provided a last tenuous connection between the passengers and those ashore as the ship began to tremble and move. Tears welled up in my eyes as the Royal Marine Band, immaculate in their white uniforms, saw us off with, 'We'll meet again, don't know where, don't know when-'. It was two weeks before Christmas.

Born into the world of high Sussex hedgerows and sunken lanes, I had become fascinated with the harsh desert landscapes and rugged mountains of the Aden Protectorate and was looking forward to some more of the same in Trucial Oman.

Travelling alone, I had no-one to give me orders on the troopship. Ignored by all of those in authority, I was free to enjoy a second, very pleasant cruise across the Indian Ocean.

Someone knew of my existence though, because when we anchored in Aden's harbour on Christmas Eve, an RAF launch came along side to collect and deliver me to where a Land Rover waited on a jetty at Steamer Point.

The deserted transit camp I was deposited in was nothing more than a cluster of dusty marquees, close enough to Khormaksar

Airport for them to be made even dustier whenever a 'plane took off.

Spending Christmas alone wasn't a very cheerful prospect. I felt that the only thing for me to do to ease the pain of loneliness was to go to one of my old haunts, the Rock Hotel in Steamer Point, get seriously drunk and blot everything out for a couple of days.

I could have taken one of the taxis waiting for customers outside the gates of Seedaseer and Singapore Lines, but with time hanging heavy on my hands, I decided to walk.

It was damned hot as I trudged along the shoreline, heading for the point where I would be obliged to leave it and take the road that skirted Maalla.

The sight of all that surf tumbling on to the sand eventually became too much for me. I needed to cool off in that water! Intense loneliness can addle the brain. Without a second thought, I removed shoes, socks, shirt and slacks; stuffing my wrist watch into a pocket containing, what was for me, a large amount of East African shillings. There wasn't a soul in sight.

It was a short swim and an expensive one. When I returned to my clothing, I discovered that everything had gone from my pockets- even my comb! Although that long stretch of shore line still appeared to be unoccupied, some opportunist had been lurking nearby, waiting to take advantage of my stupidity.

With no hope of obtaining an advance on my pay, or gaining access to my savings until well after Christmas, I returned gloomily to the transit camp and consoled myself by writing a letter to Daphne.

Good fortune smiled on me. Before the day was out, a small group of Cameronians turned up at the transit camp. Like me, they were waiting for a flight to Bahrain. Having listened to my tale of woe, they very kindly bought me a few beers at the NAAFI Club during the Christmas period, and when we finally arrived in Bahrain, insisted that I spend Hogmanay with them at their barracks, rather than stay at the 'Speedbird' Hotel.

Being the guest of a Scottish regiment at Hogmanay turned out to be an unforgettable experience!

Swooping and soaring on thermals, a Twin Pioneer aircraft took me the three hundred, or so, miles to Sharjah. Judging from what I saw while the 'plane was coming in to land, it had also taken me back two or three hundred years.

We came in low over a scruffy, straggling coastal village that had lost whatever importance it once had, when its creek silted up.

The 'Twin-Pin' bounced to a halt on hard-packed sand beside a fort with a 1930's style control tower at one end of it.

Rudyard Kipling and Lord Roberts would have both felt quite at home in the Trucial Oman Scouts camp. It appeared to have been left over from the days of the Raj. A pair of ancient cannon stood in front of the verandahed HQ building. The parade ground (more hard-packed sand) was delineated by white painted stones and the billets were straight out of 'Gunga Din'.

Old Sharjah

'Replete with stingrays and sinister snakes
A poisonous sea lapped up against
A salt encrusted stagnant shore.
Suspended fish hung drying there.
Tainting the overheated air –
Malodorous vapours under a ruthless glare.
Adobe-walled dwellings, mosaic-tiled floors,
Cooling towers and compounds
With scorpion-locked doors.+
A straggling town with barasti-roofed souk++;
Gold, silver, myrrh and a lantern wick.
Camelus Dromedarius and a camel-stick,

+Cast iron locks shaped like scorpions. Removing the tail locked the door.
++ Market, roofed over with palm fronds.

**With fellow Bollywood film fan, Cpl Gordon Nunns {R}
typically, he is wearing a shemagh and aghul more suitable
for a sheikh than a member of the TOS.**

I had already made a couple of irrational decisions in my young life. Now I had left the sybaritic pleasures of Hong Kong and journeyed to this desolate, furnace-hot place. I could hear my father's voice saying,

'You never bloody learn, do you!?'

My orders were to report directly to the commander of the TOS, the legendary Colonel Stewart Carter.

Looking for all the world like the famous, 'stiff upper lip' Hollywood actor, C Aubrey Smith, the colonel's powerful personality filled his office like a live thing. He welcomed me to the force and informed me bluntly that I was 'on my own'. His responsibilities lay with the Arab soldiers. He expected, indeed, demanded that British volunteers carry out their duties efficiently and took care of themselves. If they failed to do so, they wouldn't last long in the TOS.

Deeply impressed by Colonel Carter, I left his office; scarcely believing that a CO had taken the trouble to personally welcome a lowly lance-corporal to his unit.

The occupants of Billet 306 lifted my spirits. With one or two exceptions, here was a group of remarkably civilised junior NCOs. It's true to say that they were a cut above most of those I had encountered in the army so far. I soon discovered that this could be said about virtually all of the British volunteers. Although their number was to increase quite rapidly during the mid 1960's, we were a bit thin on the ground during my time with the force.

The Trucial Oman Scouts attracted the eccentric, the ever so slightly mad, the wild and the downright reckless. They possessed the capacity and strength of character to remain good-humoured while carrying out their duties under extremely difficult conditions. When the drink flowed, which it often did, punch-ups were not for them. Abrasive wit and risky stunts were more their style when they were 'in their cups'.

As for myself; well, I felt yet again that I was merely an

'extra'. This time I was standing on the sidelines in one of those sprawling, Alexander Korda movies set in the old British Empire.

Negotiating Dune Country

Eccentric? Gordon Nunns went to the trouble and expense of importing what, at the time, may well have been the only bicycle in the whole thirty thousand square miles of the Trucial States. Gordon was quite content with riding his bike around the camp. He had to be, because there was nothing but deep sand beyond the gates. In those days there wasn't an inch of tarmac road in the whole territory, or any other kind of road for that matter. Mostly, one made one's own track when travelling to the out stations or when on any sort of operation.

Gordon and I both had an interest in films. You may have already noticed that about me. As a consequence, although British personnel were virtually on curfew after dark, we would make our way to what passed for an open-air cinema in Sharjah. Simple in the extreme, it consisted of a few rows of wooden benches and a crude frame upon which a temporary screen could be suspended. Some sort of generator, brought in on the back of a truck that had seen better days, powered the projector. Trying to look as 'Arab' as possible, Gordon and I would buy our one rupee tickets, the Trucial Oman used Indian currency at the time, and watch endless Bollywood movies, scarcely understanding a word that was being spoken, but enjoying the visual drama, comedy and inevitable song and dance routines. We became fans of I S Johar, Raj Kapoor, and the singing voice of Lata Mangeshkar. Now and again, we were spotted as being Kafirs-Infidels and forced to beat a hasty retreat as those we'd offended, simply by being there, waved camel sticks about and roused the rest of the audience against us. 'Run like hell' was the order of the day.

Apart from the short time I'd spent in Hong Kong, and before that, the few months I'd served at Barnard Castle, I'd had little opportunity to practice whatever skills I possessed as an officers mess chef. History repeated itself, because I was never given the opportunity to do so in the TOS. The officers maintained their tradition of employing Arab cooks, so I was promoted to the rank of corporal and given the job of running the sergeants' mess kitchen, instead.

The 'kitchen' turned out to be little more than an ill-equipped shack with walls made from the wood and leaves of the date palm, commonly known as 'Barasti', through which the sand blew freely. The building, which looked as though it would collapse if anyone leant on it, had a galvanised roof on which one could quite easily fry the proverbial egg in the heat of day.

I had learned to be inventive with composite rations while serving in Aden. This small talent, together with an intermittent supply of fresh food, flown in from Bahrain, kept the ebullient bunch of senior NCOs reasonably happy. My assistants were a Goanese man and an Arab boy. We got on well together. The Goanese, whose name I'm ashamed to say I have forgotten, sometimes invited me back to his home in Sharjah. He had a charming wife and two delightful children. They lived in dire poverty, so I was always moved by their kind hospitality.

In the recent past, the man had suffered the pain and humiliation of being publicly flogged whilst strapped to the siege cannon that stood outside the Sheikh of Sharjah's palace. Having been caught stealing something or other, he was lucky not to have had one of his hands amputated. The theft had been an act of sheer desperation. One of his children had become seriously ill and he was attempting to raise enough money to buy some antibiotics for her.

One of the sergeants kept a goat in a purpose-built compound. It was missing when he returned from a trip up country. Some of his friends had thought it would be a great joke if they turned the animal into a curry. When he'd returned, they'd taunted him about this. The aggrieved sergeant kept his powder dry. A couple of days later, he gained his revenge by driving a panic-stricken donkey into the crowded mess.

'Curry that, you bastards,' he yelled, as it careered about knocking over tables and chairs and creating general chaos.

Whenever I was free to do so, I took the opportunity to travel about the Trucial States. I preferred taking part in a desert exercise or acting as a volunteer pay roll guard on trips to the out stations.

How fortunate I was to be able to take part in the rest and recreation trips to Abu Musa! Virtually deserted, this remote island was located in the approaches to the Straits of Hormuz.

Bombardier Hopkins was adamant! Only a fool suffers discomfort when he can avoid it, so there was no way he was going to Abu Musa for a long weekend without taking his bed with him. Sleeping on the ground, wrapped in a couple of blankets, or lying on a charpoy, the bottom of which was apt to rest on stony ground, was not for him. He wanted to take the bed out of his billet and that was that!

It was duly loaded onto a Bedford along with supplies sufficient for the five of us. We bounced our merry way to the quay opposite the officers' mess in Sharjah where the dhow, 'Al Qaid', awaited us with its Arab crew.

With everything stowed, and the bed standing proudly on deck, we were soon enjoying the pleasures of a dhow trip. The sea was calm, the sun shone and the fish gave themselves up to our hand lines. Using a fire built within a cut-away oil drum, I quickly converted some of them into an almost edible curry. As we ate, we watched a school of sleek porpoises flashing ahead of the 'Al Qaid', slicing their way through the phosphorescent sea.

The change in the weather came remarkably quickly. One minute all was plain sailing, so to speak, the next, we were plunging through a considerable swell. There was no rain, but the wind increased its strength as we approached Abu Musa, making it too dangerous for us to attempt to take the dhow anywhere near the stone jetty. That, incidentally, had been constructed by Germans before the First World War when they were mining red ochre on the island.

We anchored offshore, hoped it would hold, and waited.

The stormy conditions continued unabated, so we spent the night aboard the dhow. As darkness fell, a plague of wildlife emerged from its woodwork. The boat was soon swarming with cockroaches and other insect life as we lay on its pitching deck, trying to get some shuteye. The guy who'd brought his bed with him was literally above all this– he was rocked to sleep, undisturbed, on his own, firmly anchored, bed!

Putting to one side that tempting cliché, 'It was a dark and stormy night' I resort to 'Came the dawn'.

With a huge swell still running, our sensible and experienced Arab crew still refused to approach the jetty. We wanted to get on to that island!

Our eyes fell upon the tiny rowboat that had trailed in our wake, at the end of a rope, all the way from Sharjah. Rising and falling on a heaving sea we brought it alongside. The bed was lowered on ropes until it straddled the small craft, then two or three of us swarmed down to it.

Well overloaded, the rope, I suppose I ought to call it a hawser, was released and we were swept towards a tiny wedge of beach at the foot of a crumbling cliff. Boat, bed and crew were dumped like flotsam on the sand by a contemptuous wave.

After unloading the wretched bed, two brave souls made the difficult return journey to the dhow, in order to bring back our supplies and the remainder of the party. They made a similarly exciting trip to shore.

Hauling the bed to the top of that cliff was no easy task, so it was a triumphal moment for us when it stood in all its glory on the island of Abu Musa.

Shades of Coral Island! Apart from the remains of a short length of narrow gauge railway track and some abandoned wagons, once used to bring red ochre from the quarry to the jetty, there was no hint of human habitation there. The island belonged to the lizards and seabirds. We borrowed it and spent a few days swimming, fishing and climbing to its highest point, Mount Halva, which, at only four hundred feet high, hardly deserves its title.

RSM Henderson was given a Christmas present. After a little bit of bribery, the RAF guards were persuaded to allow a small aircraft, I forget what type, to be pulled from the airfield in the middle of the night. It was parked, festooned with Christmas greetings, as close to his billet door as possible, so that he would discover it when he woke up on Christmas morning.

After learning that a small unit of British paratroopers was out in the desert, five or six of us got together and decided to raid their camp.

Their exact position having been obtained by some means or other, we 'acquired' a vehicle and set off to find them. All we had to do was infiltrate their camp at night, write the letters TOS all over their vehicles, using sticks of chalk, and get out again.

Our simple strategy was to split up, get as close as possible to the paratroopers' laager, wait for darkness- and go in.

Two cheerful, armed to the teeth, hitch-hikers we found yomping across the desert while we were on our way to our unofficial night raid on the para camp.

I crawled along a shallow wadi to within about fifty yards of the target. They had circled their vehicles and two guards had been posted. Thoughts of wagon trains waiting for the Indians to attack crossed my juvenile mind. Night fell, but the moon was too bright for my liking. I didn't stand a chance of crossing the fifty yards to their perimeter without being seen. The guards were circling the camp in opposite directions, stopping to exchange a few words as they passed each other. I made a decision when their paths crossed and they stood talking together. I stood up, urinated, then, with most of my face wrapped in camo, I strolled straight into the camp as though I belonged there. The guards ignored me; but not when I crouched down in the darkness, hidden away, beside a Land Rover and attempted to write TOS on one of its doors. I didn't think to lick the stick of chalk; consequently, it made a hideous screeching sound as I attempted the downward stroke of the letter T on the metal work, bringing the guards rushing over. I stood up rather hastily when I heard them cock their Sterlings.

'Good evening,' I said, in the best plummy accent I could muster.

Although the paras muttered dire threats about what they would like to do to me, they left me alone. Paddy Farelly and John Ashworth were also captured. Ashworth had a rifle butt rammed painfully into his guts. He wasn't happy about it. The officer in charge provided us with mugs of tea and kept us bottled up in a tent until the moon was down then threw us out.

We had to cross a low range of hills to get to where we'd left the one-tonner. With no moon to light our way, it was a difficult hike. A lot of swearing and cursing could be heard as one or the other of us stumbled over rocks, fell into gullies or encountered thorn bushes.

When we re-joined the remaining members of our little expedition, we found that while the paras had been busy with us, they had been busy too; writing 'TOS' on everything they could find, before strolling back to the lorry in the moonlight and enjoying a 'brew-up'. They had been thoughtful enough to flash the vehicle's headlights from time to time, in the hope that we were out there somewhere and it would help guide us in. It had.

Towards the end of my tour, it looked to me as though the TOS was in danger of becoming as 'regimental' as any traditional British army unit. Unappealing concrete barrack blocks had been built outside the old camp. To a certain degree, their single rooms broke up the, 'we're all in it together', camaraderie that existed in the original rough and ready camp. A new style commander had arrived, together with a punctilious RSM. One thing was certain, there would be no chance of him taking over from me to finish digging a rubbish pit out in the desert, as RSM Henderson had done on a fiercely hot day, after I'd ignored his advice to put my shemagh on, and had been overcome by the heat. I was only 'out' for a minute or two, but when I came to my senses in the shade of a tent; there he was, digging away – and there were no recriminations afterwards!

A Medal Award Parade in 1961. Political Agent, James Craig, shakes hands with the Sheikh of Sharjah.

Coming in for a ration drop during an operation

Love conquers all, they say. It certainly conquered me when I first met Daphne on my mid-tour leave! She arranged to meet me off a train at her local station. I had this romantic vision of myself, the bronzed young hero returning home from foreign parts, emerging from a cloud of steam and engine smoke and into the arms of a beautiful girl waiting for me on the platform. It wasn't quite like that.

For one thing, it was an electrified railway line, so away went the steam and smoke - and for another- the platform was deserted when I alighted. Daphne was late because she'd been unable to decide what dress to wear! The only thing I'd got right in my vision was that Daphne was breathtakingly beautiful.

First Meeting

'We walked beside burgeoning hedgerows
Under an English August sun,
She with tolerant amusement
Allowing my braggart tongue to run on;
But it was my heart that raced far ahead of us
As we arrived at her garden gate;
For I knew with an utter certitude
That here was my love, my life, my fate.'

Four more years were to pass before we married.

Back with the TOS, my twenty first birthday was well celebrated! Someone had a guitar. A rough and ready double bass was constructed out of a large box, a length of wood and some stiff wire. The timpani section was provided by an oil drum and various bottles and cans. With beer being the creative force, we made a lovely noise!

I remember – I remember: a desert landscape being transformed into a brief floral delight after rare rainfall. I see swarms of locusts darkening the sky. The unfailing hospitality of the Arabs one encountered along the way. They, and much more besides, linger on in my mind. A small group of tribesmen in some far-off place I was visiting, unselfconsciously entertain themselves by performing a traditional knife dance to music played on a wind-up gramophone. A camel caravan silhouetted on the horizon.

I wander away from a night camp until it is out of sight, then stand beneath an enormous canopy of stars, listening to the silence, while imagining in that fanciful way I have, that I might be the first European to visit the spot. But most of all, I remember the comradeship of my fellow Trucial Oman Scouts;

it exists still.

I may have made service in the TOS sound too pleasurable. This is because I have no wish to dwell on the unrelenting climate, the occasional dramas and dangers, the bed bugs, salt water showers, lack of fresh water in general, and battling against the eternal desert on practically every journey one made. I could also mention, among other things, the grim, archaic working conditions for any self-respecting chef, the ever encroaching sand, the monotonous diet and the total lack of female companionship; although one senior NCO temporarily solved this last problem for himself by smuggling an air hostess from Bahrain into a desert outpost!

Then there were the flies;

'Oh, little fly upon the wall,

Ain't you got no folks at all?

Ain't you got no mum and dad?'

SMACK goes the hand----

'Then die, you bastard!'

The Foreign Office, I believe, were thinking ahead. They knew the old days were fading fast. Oil was just beginning to flow in large quantities. The Trucial States would become rich. A larger and more fully equipped force would soon be necessary to help police the region. The wonderfully wild, buccaneering days were practically over. Informality and self- regulation began to disappear. The TOS was becoming a bit too 'regimental' under the auspices of Colonel Bartholomew and RSM 'Tex' Mutter. They began holding parades and having inspections, for heaven's sake!

With a mixture of sorrow and relief, I decided not to sign on for a second tour.

6

A 'No- Brainer'

I was offered a choice of two postings. I could either become a shift NCO in the kitchens at Shepton Mallet Military Prison, or act as personal chef to the GOC, Wales District, Major General Frisby; living and working in a fine house, with lawns sweeping down to the River Wye, four miles from Builth Wells. To use modern parlance, it was a 'No-Brainer'.

In a very bizarre contrast to the life I'd been living, I was soon dealing with freshly caught salmon, hares and shot-riddled pheasants, brought in to the kitchen and slapped on the table by a dour, Welsh gamekeeper, or waiting for the general's wife to press a button in the dining room. It activated a bell in the kitchen to notify me it was time to put the cheese soufflés in the oven! It was a far cry from cooking chapattis on hot stones and drinking brackish water from a goat-skin bag.

Jugged Hare

Paunch the hare, reserving its blood for later use. Remove the intestines, clean, then skin the hare as one would a rabbit and cut into portions. Marinade the portions in 175m red wine, three cloves, one bay leaf and a tsp of allspice. Leave overnight.

Remove the portions, dust them with seasoned flour, then shallow fry the pieces in duck fat. Transfer to a casserole dish and add a bouquet garni, two chopped onions, 175g bacon lardoons, the zest of a lemon and a little of the marinade. Season and cover with chicken stock. Bring to the boil. Transfer to the oven and cook for 2 ½ hours, or until tender.

Remove the hare, onions and bacon with a slotted spoon and

keep hot on a warmed serving dish. Discard the bouquet of herbs and the cloves. Melt about 15g of butter in a small saucepan and stir in a tablespoonful of flour. Gradually add the cooking liquid. Mix until thickened. Stir in the hare blood, a couple of tablespoons of wine and some redcurrant jelly. Mix well and adjust the seasoning if necessary. Pour the sauce over the hare and serve with extra redcurrant jelly. Lovely- if you can catch the hare in the first place!

Mice will play while the cats are away- in our case, the cats were at Cheltenham or Chepstow races.

At those times, with nothing to do and nowhere to go, I was bored enough to resort to splashing about in the general's bath; making free with his shampoo and lotions while singing my heart out, using the bathroom as an echo chamber. Another diversion was using the house's fire escape equipment as a play thing. The device in question looked very much like a fire hose. It was attached to the wall of a second floor corridor, adjacent to a window. The batman and I would take turns in using it. After fastening a spring-loaded belt around my waist, I could jump straight out of the window and be lowered safely to the ground.

Once there, unfastening the apparatus would allow it to snap straight back to the window, allowing the batman to have his turn. Then it was a race round the house, through the door and up the stairs to have another go! Leaping straight out of that window was the main attraction!

There was always an element of risk attached to our antics. At times, there was no doubt we would have been done for if the general had returned home unexpectedly.

Bored again, the batman and I decided we would borrow the large skiff General Frisby kept in a boat house. Neither of us had any experience of handling boats and we failed to take in to account the speed of the River Wye's current in mid-stream.

After a few clumsy strokes of the oars we lost control of the boat. Away we went, helpless and hopeless, as the sturdy vessel sped down river, turning this way and that, while we clung on for dear life.

The skiff finally grounded on a bend, leaving us in a bit of a quandary as to how we were going to get the thing back to the boat house before the general returned home.

The answer was to push it! Unsuitably dressed in jackets and slacks, shirts and ties, and up to our waists in the cold, wet stuff, we shoved and heaved the skiff several hundred yards up river. We finally got it back to where it belonged. Phew! We didn't try that again!

Fifteen years later, together with my wife and children, I followed the course of the Wye from Builth Wells to Chepstow via Tintern.

Being self-taught does not come close to having a classical education, so I could not begin to emulate William **Wordsworth's Lines written a few miles above Tintern Abbey, as I sat on a hillside, seeing what he saw. The best I could do was grasp the nuances contained in his verses and relate to the nostalgia he felt.

'Five years have passed; five summers, with the length
Of five long winters! And once again I hear
These waters, rolling from their mountain springs-'

The year at General Frisby's house passed quickly. I provided the Frisby's and their guests with daily tucker, the occasional posh dinner, and nibbles for their cocktail and garden parties. I also took every opportunity to visit Daphne and her family at their home in Kent.

It was a long haul, there and back, with only a forty eight hour pass in my pocket. Hitch hike to Newport; Newport to

Paddington; across London to Victoria Station in order to catch the Maidstone train. Delay leaving Daphne until the last possible moment, reverse journey; hitch a lift or walk overnight from Newport to the general's house, arriving in time to cook his scrambled eggs on toast. Looking back, I find it hard to believe that I made such incredible marches; passing through silent, ghostly Abergavenny, Crickhowell and Brecon; reaching Erwood at dawn, if I was lucky. On one occasion, I called in at the barracks at Crickhowell at four o' clock in the morning. I had just about persuaded the duty driver to give me a lift, when the duty officer appeared. After I'd explained what I was doing there, he said,

'You got yourself in this mess, corporal, so you'll have to get yourself out of it, won't you?'

Then he had me thrown off the premises!

Early one wintry Saturday morning, Daphne and her father were driving through snow, on their way to the village, when they saw a dark figure carrying a suitcase, stumbling towards them on the country lane.

'Where does that idiot think he's going on a morning like this? Oh, it's Terry!'

These forced marches of mine came to an end when General Frisby somehow got wind of them. Much to his driver's disgust, he was ordered to meet me at Newport Station each time I returned from leave. He had to get out of his nice, warm bed to do so.

After the general was posted to a NATO unit in Oslo, I spent my last few months in the army, working as a shift NCO at the Cambridge Military Hospital in Aldershot. I had come full circle; ending my service less than a mile from where it had begun.

I managed to catch a severe dose of mumps while I was there.. Not funny in an adult.

'Don't worry, corporal,' the doctor said, cheerfully, as I lay in bed in an isolation ward, 'You're still firing on one piston!'

Happy in that knowledge, I left the army and signed on for life with Daphne

We enjoyed a traditional village wedding before setting off for Barcelona; journeying there by boat and train.

Typical of the ending to many a movie, the hero had overcome adversity; 'found himself', won the hand of a beautiful girl- and could have sailed away into the sunset with her if the captain of the Dover-Calais ferry had obliged us by steering a little bit more to starboard!

We had rejected a Thomas Cook agent's offer of stopping overnight in a hotel near **Evry, a suburb of Paris; preferring the romance of a sleeping compartment on the overnight train to the Spanish border at Port Bou.

While crossing the Camargue, a rather arrogant conductor I took the opportunity to practise my French on, pointed out that one only uses the word **'tu' as a form of address if one is on intimate terms with whoever it is one is talking to. When one is addressing a comparative stranger, it's 'vous' I disagreed, but he was the Frenchman, so I bowed to his superior knowledge.

At Port Bou, we crossed over from France to Spain on foot, then boarded a rattletrap train that rocked and rolled its way to Barcelona.

A Happy Beginning

On honeymoon with Daphne, my heart sang. I became poetic, but the poem, Daybreak, by Stephen **Spender, best describes how I felt. If you are interested, you will have to look it up yourself; the copyright holders wanted me to jump through too many hoops before they would allow me to reproduce it here. 'Ivory Tower' stuff.

We journeyed to the mountains behind Barcelona, visited the shrine of the Black Madonna, then climbed, hand in hand, through woods to a cloud-shrouded peak. With nothing to see, we ran back down to the monastery, laughing all the way.

Our marriage proved to be a perfect combination. While I have my head in the clouds, Daphne has both feet planted firmly on the ground. Fifty years later, I was to write:

'The hand that once held mine

On misty Montserrat;

With ten thousand tasks completed,

Remains a girl's hand,

As sweet to hold

As when we stood together

On the threshold.

During the journey home I came to regret my extravagant spending. I was flat broke again! Credit cards and ATM's being rather thin on the ground at the time, Daphne and I were obliged to survive for twenty-four hours on one orange and a bar of Toblerone!

We took up residence in a furnished flat in leafy Earlham Grove, in Forest Gate. The landlady and her husband lived on the ground floor of the house. She was waiting for me in the hallway one morning, to complain,

'I don't know what you and your wife were getting up to last night, Mr. Ward, but the chandelier in my dining room was going round and round!'

What was a happy beginning for me is also a happy ending to this part of the book

7

Brothers and Old Comrades

In 1970, my brother, Owen, or Harry (he preferred to be called by his middle name) went to see his bank manager in Crawley, West Sussex. He required a loan to help buy some land and create a market garden. The manager refused to lend him the money, telling him that he should settle down and get used to the fact that he would always be a farm labourer. That bank manager must have been related to those gentlemen who stole my education from me! Infuriated by the response to his request, Harry and our brother, Mick, took their families to Australia under the £10 immigration scheme I mentioned.

Mick having inherited our father's nomadic tendencies, embarked his family on a two-year tour of the Australian outback in a converted 'bus. While he worked on a myriad jobs: mining, sheep farming, long haul lorry driving, etc, his children were educated by radio. It seems to have worked. One of them became a schoolteacher, another currently works in a key position at Sydney Airport and the third is a senior executive in Australia's packaging industry.

In the outback, bungalows, and even houses, can be uplifted in their entirety and transported to another site.

Using his massive low-loader, Mick was doing just that for a customer.

Completely alone and miles from anything like a road, he attempted to negotiate his way through a deep gully. Almost inevitably, the bungalow became jammed between its rock walls. Mick had only one option.

When he finally delivered the building, the customer wanted to know what had happened to its verandah.

'I had to saw it off, mate,' Mick told him. 'You'll find it in the lounge room.'

**Mick Ward (ex Royal Sussex Regiment)
on ANZAC Day**

Harry eventually owned a house and several acres of land. After planting countless numbers of trees in the vicinity of the town of Gunnedah, he won the 'Greening of Australia' award. He also founded the Australian Goldwing (Motorcycle) Club and was its life president.

After he was killed in a tragic accident, it emerged that he had been quietly helping members of the scattered communities in his area, on many fronts, and over many years. As a result, the bridge crossing the gully where he was killed, was named after him. Gunnedah High School also honoured his memory by naming their new sports ground, The Harry Ward Oval. His portrait hangs in a prominent position in the school hall. About four hundred people attended his funeral. Harry's grave can be found in a 'Bush Cemetery' near to the settlement of Curlewis.

Owen Harry Ward

In 1989, I established the Trucial Oman Scouts Association. The original esprit de corps lives on. It is demonstrated every year at our splendid reunions, our Arab headgear, in the form of a shemagh and aghul, attracting a good deal of attention during the Remembrance Sunday Parade at the Cenotaph.

Trucial Oman Scouts Veterans

Remembrance Sunday

'As we form up on Horseguards
And the bands begin to play
I'm back in the Radfan, straightaway,
'Stood to' and watching tracer
Arc its way across a darkening sky.
'This is glorious!' my young heart cries;
Shouting down an older hand
Who, more aware of mortality than I,
Has no burning wish to die.

My rifle butt is rammed against my shoulder-
But what's that I hear
Ringing out above the rattle of the Browning?
Oh, yeah. I'm wheelchair bound on Whitehall
And the veterans are singing.'

8

The Grub Game versus the Grub Street Game

Thoughts of writing an autobiography entitled 'Adventure in
the Grub Game' have crossed my mind. It would relate how I
rose, if that's the word for it, from being a skivvy in a small
hotel to a university's, award winning, Head of Catering
Services {forgive the ego}. That, however, would be a sadder
task for me to undertake than writing, 'Adventures in Grub
Street', an autobiography describing my life as a hack reporter,
and how I became a successful novelist. As that is not possible,
I console myself with the thought that having one's novels
rejected by publishers and their agents over and over again,
means my writing must have some merit! Haven't they also
rejected everything from 'Animal Farm' to 'Zen and the Art of
Motorcycle Maintenance'?

Spending years in the catering industry has made me fussy about
food.

The Ubiquitous Pea

The ubiquitous pea;
The ubiquitous chip,
Served together they give me the pip.
I lean more towards beans,
You know, haricot verts
Put them on my plate
And we're getting somewhere

Add a filet mignon
And my heart fills with song,
I simply can't wait for the old dinner gong.
'Eat up your greens' may be good, sound advice,
But cabbage and kale will never entice
If they're cooked to death

In a pot full of water,
Instead of tossed in a wok
With thyme and hot butter.

Offer me 'addock
And I'll make a quick dash,
To a fishmonger I know
Who'll sell me sea-bass.

You may think I'm too finical
About the food that I choose;
But I'll drink almost anything
When it comes down to booze!

I'm afraid my father's dream of total freedom: 'We'd be better off living in the middle of a bloody great wood,' was just that, a hopeless dream. The long arm of officialdom and regulation now reach deep into the greatest forests, jungles and deserts of the world, as we render more and more of ourselves unto the petty Caesar's who rule over us. The human race has become fenced in. For the rule makers, it is still just a matter of providing the same old 'Bread and Circuses' to keep the masses quiet. The circus now comes in the form of ever-larger television screens; pouring out what is more often than not, salacious rubbish; keeping people glued to their seats all over the world.

No more the nomad.

The British Army has changed, too. A great soldier; one I was privileged to call my friend, Colonel Harold 'Geordie' Dee MBE, visited Catterick Camp when in retirement. While watching new recruits being put through their paces on the parade ground, the drill sergeant approached one of the soldiers and said to him, most politely, as he reached out to straighten the man's tie, fasten a button, or some such thing,

'Excuse me, soldier. I am obliged to touch you.'

WHAT!? The 'orrible, scruffy article should have been made to double round the parade ground several times while carrying his rifle at high port!

Geordie, who wanted to call his biography, 'Khazis I Have Known'! was a great travelling companion, as I discovered, when, together with other TOS veterans, we were invited back to the seven sheikhdoms, now transformed, in startling fashion, into the United Arab Emirates. During the visit, I found myself in the surreal situation of being called forward by minions in the president's palace, to receive the order of the Al Qasimi Tower from the hands of Sheikh Zayed bin Sultan al Nahyan, the founding father of the UAE. An undeserved 'gong' if ever there was one!

We all enjoyed remarkable and unforgettable hospitality during the ten day visit. It saddened me, though, to see large areas of desert demeaned by being fenced off and criss-crossed by motorways. Smart hotels perched on top of old, familiar mountains, better known to us as 'jebel', could be reached by good roads without effort. There seemed to be no shortage of fresh water, either!

Perhaps it's so for every passing generation, but it's the end of the world as we knew it; with the possibility of a darker one looming for our grandchildren. I'm afraid the meek do not inherit the earth and the western world appears to have grown both weak and meek.

'Ex-patriota'

The sump's smashed and the guide's absconded.
Now, only the soft sound of my own seared feet,
Shuffling through the Hadhramaut sand,
Breaks a silence so complete,
It stultifies my mind.

The sight of a skittering skink
And the twisting trail of a venomous craik,
Serve only to intensify my sense of isolation.
If only a whispering wind could bring me
The aroma of hot ghee,
Risen invisibly from the cooking pots
Of nomadic men, who, bound by desert law,
Would offer their hospitality.

But even the merest zephyr
Has been burnt up by the sun;
So I must struggle on towards those ochre striations
Shimmering on the distant horizon.

For beyond that challenging barrier, and westerly,
Lies my self-imposed destiny.
Duty and obligations command I return
To a homeland brought low by braying politicos;
And a people become more Ovus Aries
Than Panthera Leos.

It's an imperative I'm to find harder to bear,
When, in the lengthening rays of the Phoebus sphere,
A scattering of herds and encampments appear.

As camels drink, splay-legged, at a limpid pool,
'neath breeze-shivered palms in the evening cool,
Hawk-proud Bedu: Keffiyahs, curved khanjas, et al,
Bid me welcome. 'Aasalamu alaykum, min anya anta?' +
They proffer their honey-sweet coffee, and kabsa ++
How swiftly my inner Iago intones,
'You're saved, man; saved, and no longer alone!
So why now go home? Why now go home?'

+ 'Peace be upon you; where have you come from?'
++ A rice and meat dish with added spices

Colonel 'Geordie' Dee (standing)

While on a return trip to old stamping grounds I took the
opportunity to park myself in the Sheikh of Abu Dhabi's chair
the moment he turned his back on it.

Spouting opinions:

The British Empire is dead, and so are several of the nations we
abandoned to despots and mass murderers. By and large, those
countries described as 'emerging', are not. They are
submerging, Kalashnikovs in hand, into savagery.

This is the third time I've mentioned Empire in positive tones
in this brief, unimportant tome of mine. I base my opinion on
the obvious, not hysterical promotion of world 'freedom'. The
only freedom we gave back to those nations was the freedom to
indulge in mass murder, rape, mutilation, slavery and death from

disease or starvation. One can also add corruption on a scale their previous British rulers never came close to achieving. Have those liberal ideologues in the west no pity for the millions of women and children we have abandoned to their fate? It is incredibly crass to continue stating that those long-suffering people are better off without our civilised governance.

***

In the 1950's, the lower ranks of the army was no place for the sensitive. It was chock full of youths from back streets and rough housing estates; Paddies, Scouses, Geordies, Jocks and Taffys. Christian names went out of the window. You could be. 'Chalky'White, 'Tug' Wilson. 'Dusty' Miller, 'Spud' Murphy. Lofty-if you were below average height, or 'Short-Arse' if you were six feet tall.

During training, it didn't matter much where you hailed from if you let the side down by being slovenly. If you brought the wrath of the company sergeant major down on the whole billet, there were no expletives deleted.

Base though we common soldiers may have been, decency and civility must have resided somewhere inside our British breasts, because I never heard or saw anything of a racist nature occur while I was serving in Aden, the Persian Gulf and Hong Kong; apart that is, from soldiers 'slagging off' a qat-chewing Arab taxi driver, so hyper, he nearly drove his passengers off a causeway and into the sea!

I know a very courageous and intelligent man. He became severely disabled at an early age.

'An elaboration on remarks made by a housebound man'

'I have often seen her passing by my window
In dresses designed to caress lithe limbs.
Sometimes her tawny hair is creatively awry,
At others, salon-permed curls
Nestle against downy cheeks,
Pointing, pointing towards her sensuous mouth.

She has a way of holding her head, you know;
A little proudly perhaps, but I sense a vulnerability
That appeals to my protective instincts.
This morning, she glanced, wide-eyed, at my window.
I think she saw me;
Saw me looking at her from behind the nets.

Fortuitously, the driver of a passing, sporty coupe
Emitted a shrill, salacious whistle,
Startling her from her stare.
She gave the man a glare; then beamed a smile at him;
All red lips and gleaming teeth. She knew him!
And knowing him, raised a hand in further greeting,

Before walking on;
Unaware, I'm sure, of her provocative gait.
She did not turn her face towards my window again,
So I, in my turn, turned the Telegraph's pages.
And soon fell to imagining how the shot-silk blouse,
Illustrated in the fashion section,
Would fit and feel against her form.'

9

'Henry Gumble's Garden'

With the exception of Arthur C Clarke and John Wyndham, I have never sought out and read works of science fiction.

Here is the second of three, too tall, short stories

This piece of nonsense was inspired by the adventures Daphne and I experienced during the course of several visits we made to the Australian outback and the marvellous characters we met along the way. With my brother, Mick, acting as our guide, we have crossed the Big Sandy Desert, the Hay Plains and the Nullarbor. We have gone way beyond the 'Black Stump' and been to the 'Back o' Bourke', which is the place to be if you really want a taste of that elusive freedom some of us seek. For what it's worth, this yarn won me a 'Creative Writing' award from the University of Kent.

'Henry Gumble's Garden'

A few years have passed since the day I pushed my way in through the swing doors of the Old Drovers; glad to be out of the blinding New South Wales sun. After my eyes had adjusted themselves to the pub's dim interior I could see that some of the old drovers were apparently still there; lined up along the bar in time-honoured fashion. The only available space for me was at the far end. Thinking macho thoughts I made my way there, propping myself alongside a lanky, sun-bronzed type, who was gazing rather mournfully at his empty beer glass. They don't wait to be introduced in Oz. Being about a foot taller than me, the man was obliged to incline his head a little in order to make eye contact.

'What brings you to Dimbaroola, mate?'

'I'm here on holiday from England,' I told him; adding, because I was a bit puffed up about it, 'it's a present from my parents for doing well at Uni.'
I gesticulated to get the attention of the only female in the place – the barmaid.
'I knew you was a Pom the minute I laid eyes on ya,' the man, who was about thirty years old, said, 'how're you getting on in Godzown, then?'
'It's been great so far, thanks. I spent a couple of weeks in Sydney; then went to have a look at the outback. I've been knocking about on my own, up north – er, would you like a drink?'
His grin was like a flash of lightning. 'Good on ya. I'll have a Tooheys. What's your name, mate?
'It's Terence, but my friends call me Tup.'

I managed to order two beers from the busy, nubile girl, before continuing, 'I love your country. It's like a huge adventure playground for grown-ups. The people living in the outback are ever so friendly and hospitable; well, except for those I met in Coonabarramunga, that is.'

For a moment the man's face took on an odd expression, his rather prominent Adam's apple bobbing up and down as though he was having difficulty swallowing something unpalatable; and judging from the way he was hugging his glass, it couldn't have been the beer. 'Blimey, mate, have you been right up there?'

'Yes, I have,' I said. 'It's way beyond the back of Bourke, and not much of a place when you get there; just a few dirt streets and nowhere to stay. There used to be a hotel, but it was all boarded up when I arrived. It turned out to be a scary little town, too. Everybody, from the shopkeeper to the café owner, made it quite obvious they didn't want me around. I felt as though I was taking part in the opening scenes of one of those horror movies. Talk about 'Wicker Man'! The locals hardly said a word to me, and I didn't like the way they kept staring; so

I got out on the first post-bus that came along. The postman told me they were a pack of mongrels who preferred to be left alone.'

The Aussie clapped me on the shoulder as though he'd known me all my life. 'The postie was right about that, Tup. You didn't eat anything while you were up there, did you?'

'It's funny you should ask that. The café had a menu as long as your arm, but all I could get them to sell me was beans on toast. They said everything else was off, when it quite obviously wasn't.'

'That's just as well, mate. They did you a favour there. Look, you get 'em in and I'll tell you a story about Coonabarramunga,'

'Hello,' I thought, 'I bet he's after some free drinks; but I'll listen to what he's got to say in case it turns out to be the sort of traveller's tale I can impress my friends with when I get back home.'

Several, very bloke-ish blokes, wearing a variety of battered bush hats, were crowding noisily in on us at the bar, so I suggested that we took our drinks and sit at an unoccupied table close to the door. Although the Aussie made it obvious he was reluctant to put too much distance between himself and the beer pumps, he sighed and complied.

Pushing back his Jackaroo hat and downing half of the second beer I'd bought him, this temporary intruder into my life; who I suspected to be a bit of a con artist, pursed his lips and embarrassed the hell out of me by saying, bluntly.

'It don't take a mind reader to know what's going on underneath that dusty beanie you're wearing, mate. You'd better wait until I've told you what happened up at Coonie before you start thinking I'm a bleedin' bludger.'

I found myself spluttering in that very British manner, 'Sorry –

I didn't mean – I wasn't - .'

'Well, as long as you're happy about it, I'll start off by telling you about Henry Gumble's gladdies.'

My expectations of hearing a good yarn took an immediate hit. Gladioli?

I asked him to hang on a minute. 'I've told you my name's Tup. What's yours?'

'You're a bramah bloke, for a Pom,' he replied. 'I'll have another Tooheys.'

It was a response out of a joke museum, but I sighed and complied.

I'd better tell you right now that, on top of being what you might call, fresh off the farm, I was also not much of a drinker in those days. Four or five beers and my world would start tilting and turning at a faster rate of knots than I could cope with. Already on my third pint, I lambasted myself for being a gullible fool as I handed over another free drink.

'This stuff helps keep me sane, Tup,' the man, who looked twice as high as Mel, said; before leaning back in his chair and fixing his slightly un-nerving eyes on me. Then, revealing quite a decent command of the English language, he launched himself so confidently into his story. It sounded rehearsed.

'Back in 1970,' he began, 'after always being thought of as a bit of a raw prawn, Henry Gumble, suddenly turned into a bloke whose blood was worth bottling, by wiping the floor with the other competitors at Coonies Annual Flower Show. His ugly mug duly appeared on the front of the local, eight page rag. There he was, grinning like a shot fox, with a pot of his prize winning gladdies in one hand and a silver plated cup in the other. The other yobbos who took part in the competition behaved like heroes and shouted him pints of the brown stuff in the boozer. The ladies, though, were a different kettle of barramundi. Hilda Bentwhistle had her beak pushed right out of joint. She wanted to poke it into Henry's new shed to find out whether he'd put a bit more than sheep dag on his gladdies.

'There are rules about what you can feed 'em on,' she said, 'or if there ain't, there bloody well should be.'

Clara Simper, a raw-boned Sheila with a face like a half-broke Brumby, pitched in with her two penn 'orth. 'Yeah, have you seen his gourds this year? I'd like to get a look in that shed of his, too. Martha told me she's not allowed to go near it, and knowing her like I do, it must be the only thing that Henry has his own way about. Still, fair do's, eh, girls; even a battler like Henry Gumble don't always need permission from his missis before he puts his foot down, right?'

'Right,' they chorused,

The Aussie stopped talking for a moment and banged his empty glass meaningfully on the table; an action that made me decide that enough was enough. Hearing about some useless twit winning a prize at a flower show was hardly worth another free beer.

'I've got to be off now,' I told him.

There was that grin again. 'Now don't go all snaky on me, Tup. I've only just started to tell you what happened up at Coonie. I promise you, mate; your friends back home will love this when you tell 'em. I tell you what; let's do it on a pay as you go basis. You get one more round in, and after that, if you don't like what I'm telling you, you can make a dash for the door.'

I was still just about lame enough and tame enough to buy the beers and hear him out.

From time to time, as we go through life, we find ourselves in slightly surreal situations, don't we? It can be anything from being involved in a car crash, having a close encounter with a mugger, or looking for your name on the notice board at Uni and discovering that you've passed with honours when you expected to fail miserably. Whatever the event is, we suddenly feel encapsulated in our own little world; temporarily detached from the normal life that's going on around us; especially if we're half cut. Know what I mean?

It was one of those times in that pub. I was getting stupidly drunk, and listening to an increasingly bizarre tale told with conviction. The country and western music played on – and on; they were very keen on Dolly in Dimbaroola. Men entered and left, usually noisily; some of them interrupting the storyteller by slapping him on the back as they passed, urging him to be honest and, 'Stick to the dinkie die, blue,' or asking me, 'How's it hanging today, cobber?'

I discovered that the barmaid's name was Rita when things calmed down enough for her to come over and replace our empty glasses with full ones; which, of course, I coughed up for. The garrulous Aussie slid a hairy arm around her waist and attempted to untie the strings on her mini pinny with his teeth. An incident that fooled me into thinking that at least the man was reasonably normal.

Anyway, leaving all those interruptions to one side and for the sake of continuity, that's what I'm going to do; before he really got going, my thirsty friend removed his hat and looked reflectively at the pattern of stains on it, as though he was examining the runes.

'I think it was in '65 that Henry Gumble came back home to Melbourne,' he continued, his eyes following Rita's curvy return to the bar. 'After years of living like a bandicoot on a burnt ridge, Henry had decided to rejoin the human race. With his lack of looks and brains he had just about qualified to be a member. One of his priorities was to get married; so a few weeks after meeting Martha Croker at a garage sale, he proposed to her, and being no oil painting herself, she grabbed at him quicker than a rat racing up a drainpipe. Then, by some miracle of timing, when they got back from their honeymoon in Ballarat, they found that Henry had been left a bungalow and a bit of land close to Coonabarramunga; which, as you know, has a population of about ninety seven and is way beyond the black stump. Off they went to claim his inheritance.

Soon after landing up there, having found out that she'd swopped Melbourne for a shack in a dust hole, Martha turned sour. She turned sour and she stayed sour.

Their wreck of a bungalow, which wouldn't do the decent thing and fall down in a heap, was within 'Coo-ee' of Coonabarramunga and, although it stood in the shade of a group of coolabahs, the land around it was as dry as a dead dingo's donger. Hilda Bentwhistle's husband, Alec, reckoned it would make a beaut lizard farm if there was ever a demand for 'em.

There wasn't a lot of joy in Henry's life, and none at all in the bedroom. When he wasn't working for the county, grading dirt roads, he sweated away at home, trying to make a garden out of his two arid acres. Sad looking beans, stunted carrots, and ten to the pound pumpkins, was about all the poor bloke could grow. More in hope than expectation he collected a good many gardening tools. One Saturday morning, he had a brief encounter with Martha about 'em. She let him know, in that special way she had, that the second bedroom wasn't a bloody tool shed and any half decent bloke would stop scratching himself and build one.

After that little barney, Henry decided it might be a good idea at that. If nothing else, a shed would give him somewhere to hide. Timber wasn't a problem; it was free for the taking, out in the bush. So, throwing an axe and a saw into the back of his battered Nissan pick-up truck, he bailed out and went and found himself a stand of ghost gums.

Thinking unkind thoughts of Martha, he took hold of his axe and got straight into his tree felling role. Lumber-jacking like a good 'un in his tartan shirt, he scared the living daylights out of a wandering wombat by yelling, 'Timber!' at the top of his voice; a warning shout that was rather wasted, because the nearest other bloke was dying of thirst fourteen miles away. I mean, he wasn't actually dying of thirst, Tup, but he'd drunk his last tinnie and tossed it out of the cab window of the Semi he was lead-footing towards Alice; leaving the kangaroos coughing their guts up in the cloud of dust he was dragging behind.

After knocking himself out gathering enough timber for the job in hand, Henry slept well that night and woke up in the morning with an irresistible urge to set part of his shed into the cliff that rose up to a rocky escarpment at the end of his property. The idea had come to him in a dream, and being a chop short of a barbie, he went and told Martha his brilliant idea.

Her carefully considered response set the kookaburras laughing so hard they nearly fell out of the eucalyptus!

Henry wouldn't be put off, though. As a matter of fact, he couldn't be put off! The poor drongo didn't know it, but he was now under the thumb of something that could eat Martha for breakfast and still have room for a fried slice.

Working flat out like a snake, Henry began to dig his way into the cliff, supporting the roof with timber as he went. Half of his new shed would soon be standing in the relative cool, or so he thought. It would be great for storing his 'gladdie' bulbs and his onions – or so he thought.

When Martha paid a surprise visit to the site, she told him he'd proven to her complete satisfaction that he had fewer brains than the average galah. With a bit of luck, the whole bloody cliff would come crashing down and knock some sense into him.

Ignoring these scornful observations, Henry just kept on hacking his way deeper into the cliff, only coming to a halt when he hit a solid wall of rock.

'It's just like a wall built out of rock,' he told Martha, when he dragged his sweat soaked body back to the bungalow.

'The same stuff your head's made of, I suppose,' was her, not unexpected, reply.

Well, Tup, me old mate, it was just like a wall built of rock because it was – a wall built of rock, as Henry found out, when, sweating chunks again, he broke through into the store. In the blink of a skink's eye, his life was turned A over T. The place was piled high with what appeared to be tons of sand, but upon closer examination, the grains turned out to be shaped like tiny Smarties. Henry picked up a handful and took a sniff. No smell at all. Then, just like the lamb-brain he was, he stuck out his tongue and licked the stuff. YUCK, Tup! They tasted even worse than Martha's beef cobbler! After nearly chucking up, he opened his mouth to yell for her, but closed it again when he saw what looked suspiciously like a TV screen light up on the back wall. A weird, sausage-shaped head appeared on it. It had a nice tan, he gave it that, but the one eye, blinking between a pair of lips that would have done a dugong proud, was a bit unnerving; and, come to think of it, where were its ears – and its hair? The thing was as bald as a balloon.

'G'day, sport,' it said. 'Greetings from the planet Ovis; you received my dream message, then.'

'Ya dinner's cold,' was the less startling message Henry got when he drifted, in a trance-like state, into his kitchen a little while later.

'Good, thanks,' he said, hugging himself, as though he'd just won the Lotto. 'I'm going to need a lot of bags, Martha. I've got through that wall, I mean, rock face, and the soil behind there looks very rich. I'm going to bag it up and put it on the garden.'

From the look Martha gave him, you'd have thought she'd just swallowed a pint of lemon juice. 'You're bloody crackers.'

'Don't go near that digging, my love,' Henry pleaded. 'It might be a bit dangerous. I don't want you getting hurt.'

Of course she went berko at that. 'I'm not interested in your bloody hole in the ground! I've got me work cut out keeping red ants out of the lounge room.'

Henry bailed out again and drove like Fangio to Coonie to buy some large, strong bags.

Then, going at it like Robbie the Robot, he bagged up the strange, ghastly tasting stuff he'd discovered, and stacked it by the cliff face.

After scraping every last bit out of the store, he braced himself for the next little job.

'Bang goes my nice, cool shed,' he thought, as he tied a rope to the pit props supporting the roof of his diggings. 'I hope it's going to be worth it.'

Fastening the other end of the rope to the rear end of the Nissan, he made sure the coast was clear, then let her rip, causing a minor avalanche.

You may think Henry was a bit of a wuss for doing that, Tup, because his fortune would have been made if he could have got away with opening up his discovery to the public. Apart from anything else, it would have been on every tourists' 'must see' list. That didn't happen; because our Henry was scared stiff of the strange life-form that had appeared on the telly in that store room. He wasn't going to risk being, 'Melted to the size of that dew drop on the end of your nose if you don't do as you're told, sport.'

When, for no accountable reason, the afore said dew drop suddenly reached boiling point, leaving a painful little blister behind, Henry did as he was told. He knew which side his bread was buttered when it came to dealing with blokes from Ovis.

After bringing down the roof and completely sealing off the store from prying eyes, Henry returned to the bungalow, covered in dust and with a variety of small stones nestling in his hair like a clutch of birds' eggs.

Martha wouldn't let him into the kitchen, so he had to strip to his grundies and wait outside until she brought out a bowl of soap and water.

'If I had my way, I'd turn a bleedin' hose on ya,' she screeched. 'I told ya you'd come a gutser and that cliff would fall quicker than England's first wicket, but would ya listen? Oh no, not you! What are you going to do next? Mine for gold with a dinner fork?'

For once in his married life, Henry became defiant. 'I'm going to build my shed and store those sacks of good dirt in it,' he informed her, through a mixture of dust and soap suds.

He did, too; and you had to hand it to him, it was a ripper of a shed. When it was finished, he painted it black and filled it with umpteen bulging sacks before securing the door with a padlock the size of Tasmania.

Henry had a bumper crop of just about everything in '69. Even Martha was impressed. He'd only used up two of the bags; sprinkling their contents over his garden as per the instructions he'd received from 'Sausage Head'.

Later that year, he'd grown so much prime stuff he didn't know what to do with it, so he set up a veggie stall on the dirt road that ran past the bungalow. The locals, curious to know the reason for Henry's sudden success as a gardener, came to buy it and ask questions, but he kept mum, and as for Martha, well, she could smell money from a mile off, so she wasn't saying anything about the 'magic dirt' her old man was using.

The stall did such a roaring trade it wasn't long before Henry gave up working for the county, turned his home into a place to be proud of and bought himself a nice greengrocery business in town. Talk about dumb luck! The more of Henry's veg that Martha ate, the sweeter her disposition became, and before you could say, 'Up jumped a Jumbuck', there she was, washing the nappies of their own little ankle biter; and on my oath, Tup, she was singing away, happy as Larry, while she did it. And what's more, Coonabarramunga, although it don't welcome strangers, became the happiest, bloody near off the map, place you could ever wish for.'

My incessantly slurping friend paused and eyed his eternally empty glass.

'That's a fair dinkum ending, don't you think?'

Beer had made me bold. 'No, I don't, as it happens,' I told him. 'You haven't explained a damn thing. All I've heard from you is a load of guff about what happened before and after Henry broke through the wall, if there ever was one; and why the hell would aliens leave a pile of fertiliser hidden in the middle of nowhere in Australia?'

He waved his stinking beer glass under my nose. 'Oh, come on, Tup, you're a graduate; use your brains, can't ya?'

'I am using my brains. That's why I'm off,' I said, making a valiant effort to stand up, and, due to the fact that most of my neurons had keeled over in a drunken stupor, failing miserably.

My attempt to leave the tall story teller high and dry, as it were, was enough to scare him into thinking he was in danger of having had his last freebie of the day; so off he went again.

'All right, all right, in a nutshell, then; and I think this is worth another schooner of Tooheys'; way back, even before 'Neighbours' was thought of, blokes from the planet Ovis were doing the decent thing and travelling about the universe, using the dried droppings of the Bula bird, which is native to their planet, to make deserts bloom wherever they came across 'em. Just after they arrived in Oz, they had a bit of a blue back home and shot off, leaving a pile of the fertiliser behind. They don't like waste, so they left a sort of prescient, not all Aussies are thickos, mate, I said, prescient, communication set-up, for the first bloke to come along with an IQ low enough for them to contact and control. Apparently, they can only connect with pea brains, so Henry qualified. What's that you say? 'Bula' is Fijian for, 'Welcome'? So it might be, mate, but on Ovis it's the name of a sort of giant emu. Anyway; as I was trying to tell you, 'Sausage Head' ended his little chat with Henry by warning him that his life wouldn't be worth a brass razoo if he let on about the Bula droppings, or how he'd got his hands on 'em. He was welcome to use the stuff on his garden, but if he didn't destroy the evidence of their visit, they'd make sure he'd wind up dead in a dunny. They'd rather not have any of us Earthlings popping up to visit 'em, thank you very much; at least, not before we get a bit more civilised. If we play our cards right, we might get an invite to their Millennium Barbie in six hundred year time. As for those so-called mongrels up at Coonabarramunga, they all became addicted to Henry's produce, and apart from a side effect that can make for some rum party nights, everybody is as happy as a croc in a paddling pool at half term. Not wanting hordes of investigators and medics up there, they keep their veggie paradise to themselves; which is why everybody hides the welcome mat from any nosey bugger who turns up there like you did.'

Thrusting an empty glass at me and displaying his well-known mournful look, the Aussie added, 'And that's it, from go to whoa; now, ain't that worth a couple more beers? I've developed a taste for 'Tooheys' since I've been in Dimbaroola.'

That was it as far as I was concerned, as well. By that time, I'd not only got that reeling feeling, I'd also started to become, Mister Pugnacious Five-Pints. 'Yeah, I've notished you enjoy the stuff. It mus' be 'cos ish so cheap for you,' I slurred, somewhat dryly, if you'll excuse the pun. 'You're not getting any more free drinksh out of me, I can tell you that, MATE! You've been having me on with your ridic-lush shtory. For a shtart, how could you possibly know all those details – I may be drunk, but I'm not shtupid.'

 The long, nut-brown streak promptly aced my attempt at 'Jack the lad' pugnacity by rising up from his seat and looming over me in a threatening manner. 'You still think I'm pulling your pisser for a pint, do you, mate? Well, I don't like being called a bloody liar. I may have used a bit of poetic licence in the telling, and slagged off me poor old mum and dad a bit; but I know what I've been going on about because I happen to be Henry and Martha Gumble's little ankle-biter, all grown up, see? I didn't intend to let you in on this bit because 'Sausage Head' told my old man that he was allowed to pass his secret on to his first born son, along with the same Ovis health warning about being zapped if he ever opened his mouth about it; but it must be like father, like son, right down the line on Ovis, because he stuffed up by not banking on a no-hoper like Henry having a son with a brain. My IQ's so high the buggers can't get through to me. There's another thing I didn't intend to tell you; eating Henry's fruit and veg put everybody up at Coonie in such a state of permanent euphoria – I hope you're impressed with me intellect- that nobody cared about the bummer of a side effect. Being a bit of a rebel, I eventually got out of there and went cold turkey walkabout for several months until I broke the addiction to my dad's stuff. I haven't got rid of the side effect yet; so, if you still don't believe me, I reckon it's safe to give you a little demo. The state you're in, nobody here will believe a word you tell 'em. They'll laugh in your pink Pom face. So, if you can manage to get up on your hind legs, we'll go out the back, right now, and I'll prove to you I've been giving you the good oil. I'll show you how I can change the shape of me head until it's just like a bonza, great sausage, with one eye in the middle, no hair, no ears –' softening his voice, he added, 'and as I haven't 'ad it circumcised, yet - A PAIR OF NICE, KISSY LIPS!'

He then gave me such a frightful leer, it made my skin crawl.

Sudden fear sobered me up. As I made a panic stricken dash for the door, he shouted, - 'AND YOU SHOULD SEE WHAT THE SHEILAS' CAN DO!'

Was that a burst of laughter I heard emanating from the customers in the Old Drovers?

I'm not sure; I was too drunk, too scared and too busy running!

10

I believe in Christmas

Daphne and I eventually purchased a house in Rochester, Kent. We still live there, enjoying the city's history, architecture and hidden gems, but most of all, Charles Dickens' all-pervading presence. Until his death, I had the pleasure of assisting the great writer's grandson, Cedric Charles Dickens, in re-creating the annual Christmas Banquet and Ball as described in The Pickwick Papers. What joyous events they were! They took place in the ball room at the Royal and Victoria Hotel in Rochester, as described by Dickens in his riotous story.

At the beginning of the event, wearing the tallest toque and the longest apron I could lay my hands on, I would weave my way around the diners, holding aloft an enormous, garnished turkey.

Carrying a flambéed Christmas pudding in the same manner, I would repeat the performance towards the end of the banquet, receiving great applause as I did so.

As the guests departed they were obliged to stir the pudding mixture in preparation for the following year's event.

There has been a threat to build an international airport on the Isle of Grain. Out there on those marshy flatlands, in the quiet of a misty evening, one may encounter more than will o' the wisps. The spirits of the escaped convict, Magwich, Joe Gargery, the blacksmith, and even that of young Pip, can easily begin to haunt one's imaginings as the sun dies and the peewits cry. Here, with apologies to CD, is a Christmas story…

Mr. Pickwick's Flight of Fancy

Mr. Samuel Pickwick would not be browbeaten, not even by a forbidding apparition.

'You, sir, are in the wrong story,' he said firmly.

'Indeed I am not, sir,' protested the Spirit of Christmas Future, 'I go where I wish, sir.
'Well, I wish you'd go, sir! What the devil do you want with me?' Pickwick spluttered.

'I would rather you did not mention that personage in my presence, sir; it displays very bad taste, if I may say so.' The extremely civilised ghost said, mildly. 'Come along, I have something to show you.'

Pickwick grew greatly alarmed and rather breathless when the ghost took him by the sleeve. He suddenly had the sensational sensation of viewing the sun, moon and stars rising, setting and swirling rapidly about the heavens all in the blink of an eye.

'Where on earth are we going?'

'To the year of our Lord, two thousand and thirty five, sir. You have been expressing some disappointments recently about the age in which you live, have you not?'

'I only said that the old days are gone forever--,' Pickwick began.

'I know, sir. My job is to restore contentment to your life. You are a good fellow and that is why I have, for the time being, left the ES business to the Spirit of Christmas Past. Steady now, we're coming in to land.'

Samuel Pickwick arrived with a thump into the unforgiving dimensions of seat 32c aboard Gradgrind Airlines, flight GG4U. He was feeling more than a little strange and had been since his ghostly escort had evaporated, after sniggering and saying in an oddly guttural tone of voice, 'I'll be back,' leaving Pickwick to descend, literally out of the blue and into a monstrous aircraft standing on a runway at Charles Dickens Airport.

The complex dominated, not to say, overwhelmed, this once isolated, marshy area of North Kent. The villages of Cliffe and Cooling were no more, and Allhallows, sitting in the shadow of the Thames estuary's gigantic sea defences, had become quite unholy. One thousand seat, Jumbo jets, waiting their turn to land, continually circled above a mass of brooding, box-like houses encircled by road systems

Pickwick may have been a man adrift out of his own time but he recognised the faces and knew the names and character of every other passenger on the aircraft, even though he had never met a single one of them!

There was the stone-faced Mr. Nickleby, chatting away to the fawning Uriah Heep. Next to them sat the tightlipped Murdstones. Wilkins Micawber, with three or four young children clinging to various parts of his anatomy, struggled to his seat. Then Bill Sikes and Magwitch came aboard. Bearded and in chains, they glowered, red-eyed, at anyone who dared glance at them.

Adopting the policy that discretion was the better part of valour, Mr. Pickwick gave his shoes a careful examination as they passed by.

The Twist boy, Pumplechook, Betsy Trotwood; they were all there, even night-shirted, haunted, Ebeneezer- Ebeneezer- Snooze? No, that cannot be the fellow's surname. It must be his nightshirt that brought the word to mind. Ah! Not Snooze! 'Silly me!' Pickwick chided himself, 'It is Scrooge, indeed it is! I understand what the sprit meant by 'ES', now! Scrooge must have escaped from the Spirit of Christmas Past!'

Mr. Pickwick had no problem with naming Phillip Pirrip. He was looking just as pale and frail as all the other passengers; emanating a ghostly other worldliness and so completely ignoring Pickwick, he began to wonder if he was actually there at all. He pinched himself-hard.

'OUCH!' Yes, he was there, and still alive, but where were his own dear friends? Where were Snodgrass, Winkle and Tupman? Added to that, where was Mr. Jingle and his own manservant, the ever reliable, Sam Weller? Pickwick groaned. 'Am I to suffer this living nightmare without the support and comfort of my dear friends?'

He closed his eyes the better to think of them, only to have them startled open again by a sharp stabbing sensation in his ribs. A short, fat lady was standing by his seat, holding a toasting fork in one hand and the wreckage of an umbrella in the other. Her lank hair stuck out in all directions from beneath a ragged cap, worn at a defiantly reckless angle.

'Belt up, dearie, we're about to take orf,' she said.

To Mr. Pickwick's dismay, the creature leant over him, 'hang on, I'll do it up for ya.'

He could smell the gin on her breath as she took hold of his seat belt. The wretch caught a glimpse of the initialed badge sewn on the breast of his cutaway coat.

'Oh, so it's PC, is it? I didn't know the politically correct had formed a club. It must be a big 'un.'

Mr. Pickwick spluttered indignantly, 'political, madam? Political? I should say not! This badge denotes my membership of a most exclusive club. The renowned and greatly respected Pickwick Club! In fact, madam, I am Mr. Samuel Pickwick, himself; the founder of the aforesaid exclusive club.'

'Oh, you're 'im, are you?' Judging from her tone, she was unimpressed by his credentials. 'I've been looking for you. Come along a' me. You've got to fly this 'ere plane!'

Pickwick was appalled. 'What do you mean, madam; fly the plane?' Nevertheless he found himself rising from his seat and following her disgraceful bustle down the aisle. Various people grasped his hand or called out to him as he passed by.

'Best o' luck', Sam Weller said. His manservant had popped up from nowhere, like a Jack-in-the-box.

Upon entering the cockpit, Pickwick was vastly reassured when he examined the controls. He knew how to fly the machine! Stranger and stranger!

Within a few moments, he had it roaring down the runway and soaring up into the sky. What a thrill!

There were the Medway Towns, far below; but wait! The eponymous river that should have been snaking its course around them had broadened into an enormous lake. Why, the water was washing up against the castle walls! A single glance was enough for him to see that the entire Medway valley was inundated. Great, manmade barriers protected Rochester, Chatham and Strood from any further encroachment.

'Bless my soul!' Pickwick could not believe his eyes.

A voice in his ear said,

'That's global warming for you, sir! Those in authority would not take heed and this is the result. It's typical, sir. I said, typical!'

Pickwick examined this newcomer over his spectacles as, despite everything he tried to do to make it fly in a straight line, the aircraft insisted on circling above Rochester.

That pompous individual, the Beadle, now loomed over Mr. Pickwick.

'To duty, sir, to duty. Your identity card, if you please,'

'My identity card? I do not believe I possess such an item as that.'

'Of course you do, sir. Everyone does; and here's yours sticking out of your weskit pocket.'

The Beadle snatched up the card and scrutinised it. 'Hmmmh, Pickwick-that's a 'P' and it's Thursday, so you're legal.' He stuffed the card back into Pickwick's waistcoat pocket. This worthy gentleman wanted some answers.

'What on earth do you mean, sir, it's a 'P' so I am legal? Thursday or not, I am always legal, sir!'

The Beadle frowned at him, 'not if you're out on a Tuesday and you are a 'P', you're not. Have you forgotten the PCC rules? A's to L's is Mondays to Wednesdays and M's to Z's is Thursdays to Saturdays. Pickwick is a 'P', so you're legal today, it being Thursday, and all. It's the Population Congestion Control. PCC see? And I've just got one, Uriah Heep, by name, on a PCCC! 'im being an haitch for 'eep and it not being neither a Monday, Tuesday or Wednesday. It cost him twenty euros for a Population Congestion Control Charge!'

Mr. Pickwick gripped the controls of the aircraft and groaned again. 'Is everyone insane? I must awaken myself from this nightmare!'

The Beadle looked annoyed, 'come, come, sir. Things are getting better all the time. Anybody can go out and about on Sundays, and the opportunities for boating are himmense since the rising of the waters. Lord Beckham, the representative for the English region of the United States of Europe, is making an impact in the federal capital, New Berlin. He's allowed the public back into Windsor Castle pretty quick, since he purchased it from King Bill. Very sporting of him, don't you think?'

The Beadle's voice, although growing fainter, droned on. Pickwick caught something about how happy the royals were now they'd settled into Bleak House, in Broadstairs.

His attention was diverted by the sight of a large, white feather that was defying the laws of physics and dancing merrily up and down, just beyond the cockpit windscreen. It was as light as -as, well, as a feather, he supposed. Pickwick clung to the steering column, trying to resist the urge to sneeze.

Suddenly the cockpit became full of people. Mr. Jingle was there. Pickwick couldn't stop himself from shouting out to him,

'Look out, Jingle! PCCC! You are a 'J' and it is Thursday!' He continued to wrestle manfully with the controls, but to no avail. The 'plane began diving straight towards the castle!

'Ah, fine place, magnificent pile,' said Mr. Jingle, staring intently at the Keep. 'Frowning walls-crumbling staircases --'

'Somebody help me, pleeeaaase!' Pickwick cried out in despair.

'Barkus is willin,' Barkus is willin', intoned a voice.

A Bow Street Runner had the Beadle by his collar on the crowded flight deck.

'Your name's Bumble, ain't it? Why then, the law says that'll be twenty euros as it's Thursday.'

The Beadle cried out, 'But I'm a People Congestion Control Charge Collector; so if the law says that, then the law is a idiot, a ass!'

'No exceptions, no exceptions,' intoned the Bow Street

Runner.

'What larks, eh, Pip? What larks!' Joe Gargery sounded delighted as the great castle loomed terrifyingly close.

'It's a far, far better thing –'

As Pickwick covered his face with both hands, the soothing voice and presence of the Spirit of Christmas Future was with him.

'Come along, sir; you have seen enough. Let's get you back with your friends at Dingley Dell Farm.'

'Stop! Stop! Oh no, please stop!' The child who'd been amusing himself by tickling Mr. Pickwick's nose with a goose feather, dashed away, gurgling mischievously when the man in question suddenly woke up.

'Oh, thank you, God!' Pickwick called out in blessed relief. There were his dear friends and travelling companions, Snodgrass, Tupman and Winkle, all taking their ease. His genial host, Mr. Wardle, was looking at him with some concern Across the other side of a blazing log fire, sat the ladies, fanning themselves. They were also eyeing him, but why so disdainfully? Pickwick wailed,

'Please forgive me for calling out, dear ladies, but I have just seen the future and it is both fearful and utterly frightful!'

They turned away from him. 'Oh, heavens,' Pickwick groaned. They think I am intoxicated! How unjust! I am as sober as they are!' At that moment Mrs. Wardle emitted an extremely loud hiccup.

Mr. Jingle, hale and hearty, came to his side and began consoling him in his staccato fashion.

'Large luncheon– very. Goose, gammon, gravy, Kentish fare- all sorts, then plum pudding, pies and pickles, port wine-cheese- glass or two of Madeira - Bacchus and cornucopia - result nightmare. All's well now, old fellow- nothing to fear, nothing to fear at all.'

'But I have seen the future!' Pickwick insisted.
'Course you have - been there myself- many times,' Mr. Jingle consoled him, as did Tupman, Winkle and Snodgrass, as they sympathetically closed ranks round him.

With their presence and kindly concern reassuring him, Pickwick began to laugh, hesitantly at first and then more heartily, 'Oh, what is the use? No one will ever believe where I have been and what I have seen!' The fat boy was bearing down upon him, carrying a tray of brimming glasses. Pickwick sent up a silent prayer of thanks to the Spirit of Christmas Future. He was happy to be back in his own blessed time, safe and snug with his friends on Manor Farm in Dingley Dell, and, and what's more, here was a PC that he could delight in - for it was, was it not, an absolutely Perfect Christmas!

11

The Levelling Dust of Fate

Daphne and I paid a visit to Auschwitz while on holiday in the Tatra Mountains. It proved to be one of the most moving experiences of our lives.

Visiting Auschwitz

They have widened the road into Auschwitz.
Tourist vehicles arrive every day.
More sinister coaches were railed here once-
Whose passengers would - stay.

I was taken to view the exhibits
In those barrack-rooms from hell.
While passing the mounds of human hair,
I controlled my emotions well.
But upon seeing the murdered children's shoes
The tears fell.

Righteous rage became somewhat abated
My blood coursed a little more cold.
The camp boss was hanged there,
In the cold, open air,
On a purpose-built scaffold.

Later, I tipped the Polish attendant
She said, 'Danke schon' and, 'Bitte schon.'
It took me a moment to realize
That she had mistaken me for a German.

Adjacent to Auschwitz-Birkenau
A community has grown.
Its people have only to lift their heads
To view what man has done.
How can they sit in their homes
And drink coffee, while gossiping by the fire,

With the ghosts of three million souls,
Still hanging nearby on the wire?

They have widened the road into Auschwitz,
It's more now than, 'Raus, Juden. Schnell!'
The spear and the nail wounds are bleeding.
Tribe, Race and Nation, 'APPEL!'

There follows another shameless piece of Book Promotion

The 17th century poet, James Shirley, wrote that there was no armour against fate. I concur, and attempt to explore the concept in my novel, The Levelling Dust

A series of unavoidable minor events have led to Douglas Bowen being responsible for the death of his parents and a younger brother. While his remaining brother, Robert, struggles to make his way in the world, Douglas, serving in the army, has been posted to Korea where war is raging…

Capture and Escape

While soldiers fought and died, the Korean War peace talks at Panmounjon were being jeopardised by the failure of the protagonists to agree upon the shape of the conference table. Until that problem could be resolved, they would remain bogged down, much like many of the United Nations forces' vehicles were in the spring thaw.

For thousands of soldiers dug in on the inhospitable hills, the danger of frostbite had given way to the possibility of trench foot.

Supply: That was and had been the main factor upon which defeat or victory had rested for both sides. The North Koreans and Chinese had stretched themselves so thin and so far from their bases that they were unable to sustain their major thrusts into the south. The United Nations forces had learnt, albeit a little belatedly, that they had to take and hold the high ground in order to keep the valley roads open to the traffic of war, and that led to their own particular supply problems.

Key hills changed ownership more than a few times as one side wrested them bloodily from the other, only to lose them once more to an overwhelming counter attack. Echoes of the First World War could be found in the miles of bunkers, trenches and tunnels constructed for the preservation of life and the supply of ammunition and food. Not even the sturdiest vehicle could carry supplies to those rugged, fortress hilltops. Everything required to keep the fighting men in position was portered up to them, via the rear slopes. It was, perforce, a night-time activity that was frequently carried out under fire, with star shells hanging over the porters, and mortars exploding all around. Stores and ammunition would be carried up, and the sick or wounded soldiers brought down to where the convoys brought in the bulk supplies and removed the quick and the dead.

Douglas Bowen had survived the winter. Along with the other drivers he learnt how to keep engines running when the air temperature was twenty degrees below zero. He learnt to love space heaters, hot composite rations and the comradeship of fellow soldiers. Then there was that rich intensity of feeling as

the adrenalin flowed while he negotiated his lorry load of supplies over dangerous terrain; part of a convoy ferrying replacement troops and supplies along the shelled and mortared road that ran through the Sami Chon Valley, south of the Imjin River.

Even after the spring monsoon had washed away all traces of snow and ice from the hills, replacing it with an unexpectedly brilliant floral display, parties of soldiers with bitter memories, might be heard singing,

'On top of old Smokey
All covered in snow.
You'll all freeze your arse off.
Because it's forty below.
Your nose will get frost- bite
And so will your toes.
What else will get frozen?
The Lord only knows.
It might be your fingers,
Or it might be an ear.
But whatever else freezes,
There's only one thing to fear.
If you visit the M.O.
And he asks you to cough
Don't do as he orders
'cos your balls might drop off!'

Douglas could be just as afraid as the next man. If his vehicle
was part of a column coming under sniper fire, he would feel
fear, all right; but after surviving unscathed, he felt as though
God had missed yet another opportunity to punish him for his
sins.

News of David's death had belatedly caught up with him.
Theinformation had been sent in error to another Service Corps
man of the same name, who was serving in Malaya. Returned to
an office somewhere, it had gathered dust in a clerk's 'in tray'
for a while.

Douglas strove to picture David's face, but found it difficult to
visualise. He couldn't remember him clearly; a fact that added
to his self-loathing.

Now he confided in Jim Feltham as they squatted by their
vehicle, drinking scalding hot tea from their mess tins.

'I was just beginning to believe that I could write to my
brothers and tell them what really happened to mum and dad.

How the hell can I do that now? If it hadn't been for me, David wouldn't have been in that place when it caught fire. It all seems so bloody deliberate. One thing leading to another until that poor little devil, who never lived long enough to harm anybody, gets caught up in stuff that kills him. And I'm the - the, I know there's a word for it, Jim. What is it?'

'Catalyst, Doug. You were the catalyst. I sometimes think that the ancient Greeks were right. The Gods are up there on Mount Olympus, playing with our little lives for their own amusement.'

He looked up and down the long line of assorted vehicles drawn up by the side of a dirt road. 'See this little lot? Only quirks of fate have brought most of them here, and us too, for that matter. I'm here because an officer sprained his ankle on Otterburn Ranges. Come to think of it, you and me would never have met if that silly sod of an adjutant hadn't tripped over his own feet. We don't seem to be able to do much about most of the stuff that happens to us, except make the best of it.'

Douglas swirled the tea around the bottom of his mess tin. 'What's the point of trying to do anything if we don't have any control? We might as well just give up.'

'Giving up is not in most men's nature,' Feltham told him. 'That's what brought us down out of the trees in the first place. And, anyway, we do have some control over our lives, don't we? Good things happen all the time through our own efforts. We can work and achieve goals, get rich, get a good woman –'

'Yeah; then get called up and sent out here to get shot in the head,' Douglas finished for him.

'Perhaps,' Feltham tossed his cigarette end into the ditch, 'or maybe survive and discover that being here leads us down unexpectedly pleasant roads, and on to a life that we hadn't anticipated. Who knows? It's all one bloody, big mystery that even the brainiest bastards in the world haven't solved yet; and I doubt they ever will.'

Engines began to start up all along the line, disturbing the peace of a countryside littered with the debris of war. The civilian population made use of most of the trash left behind by troops, but there was still a sufficiency of it strewn about, to deface the landscape.

'Come on, cheerful,' Feltham said, 'you're in charge of this vehicle, so you'd better start it moving. 'The Duke of Wellingtons' are waiting for a change of socks and a copy of 'Tit Bits', up in them thar hills.'

Muddy paddy fields stretched away to their right. Feltham shouted above the din of the engine as the vehicle rocked and swayed along the rutted track.

'That's the beginning of the minefields. Do try and stay on the road, eh?'

Douglas grinned, as he wrestled with the steering wheel. 'Don't worry, Jim, the only way I want to get legless is in a bar in Tokyo!'

The road began to snake its way around the base of the hills, so they didn't see the first mortar shell take out a Land Rover, killing a Royal Signals corporal and Lieutenant Hapgood, the officer in charge of the convoy. At the sound of the detonation, Feltham snatched up his Sten gun.

'Here we go!'

They rounded the bend. The entire convoy was speeding up; everyone was under orders not to stop for anything or anyone. It had been drummed into them many times, that if they came under a serious attack, an air strike would be called up to bomb and napalm the enemy positions. Their job was to keep going if they could, and get the supplies through. Douglas floored the accelerator and passed the wreckage of the Land Rover containing two mangled corpses.

'That's one of the radios gone for a Burton, Jim!' Douglas narrowed his eyes. He was getting closer and closer to the tailgate of the three-tonner in front of them.

'Come on, mate, get a bloody move on!' In a futile gesture, he pounded on the horn. 'Bloody Sunday drivers!'

'Shall I get out and give him a push?' Feltham enquired mildly.

Before he could come back with a suitable reply the lorry in question received a direct hit. Its canopy disintegrated in a flash of flame. The stricken vehicle veered to the left, ran on for a few yards, tilted at a crazy angle as it hit the slope, then crashed back onto the middle of the road before coming to a sliding, grinding halt.

Douglas swung the steering wheel in an effort to avoid hitting the obstruction, and ploughed into the muddy ground on the right.

Feltham held his Sten gun in front of his face as a useless form of protection.

'Look out; we're in the bloody minefield!'

Douglas stood on the foot brake as the remainder of the convoy negotiated the wreckage of the mortared Bedford. Its driver and co-driver had escaped unscathed and now made a desperate leap for one of the passing tailgates, hauling themselves aboard as the vehicle accelerated away.

Despite his best efforts, Douglas was unable to prevent his lorry from sliding sideways in the foot deep mud as he brought it to a swaying halt.

A mine exploded beneath one of the rear wheels; the force almost stood the lorry on its nose. With its rear wheels spinning and the engine whining, the vehicle toppled onto its side. Douglas's head cracked painfully against the bodywork of the cab. Winded by being thrown against the steering wheel and with a sharp pain in his rib cage, he sprawled helplessly on top of Feltham. Deprived of its fuel, the engine coughed and stuttered into silence.

'Look, I'm fond of you, Doug, but would you mind getting your head out of my lap?' Feltham's words sounded as though they were being forced through clenched teeth.

Douglas managed to reach up and grab hold of the door handle. Although the effort increased the pain in his ribs, he pulled himself into a position where he could fling the door open.

'Are you all right, Jim? It looks like that Rickshaw Wallah in Hong Kong has got some relatives in Korea.'

'I do the jokes,' Feltham said, 'and no, I'm not bloody all right. My right knee hurts like hell. I've busted something, that's for sure. Help me up out of here, will you?'

Douglas made another effort. This time he hauled his torso into the open air. His appearance was greeted by the sound of Burp guns as bullets came humming and zipping over his head, persuading him to duck back into the cab.

'Pass me up that Sten, if you can manage it, Jim.' He could see part of the weapon protruding from beneath Feltham's twisted body.

'Don't be daft! you can't fight them, Doug, not on your own; and I can't help you much while I'm jammed in here with this busted leg.'

'I know that, Jim, but I might be able to hold them off for a little while. Someone will have got a message off, so there'll be an air strike on its way to sort them out.'

'Yeah, and they might sort us out at the same time if they're a bit off target.'

Feltham scrabbled for the weapon and handed it up by its muzzle. 'You're going to get us both killed, you daft bugger.'

Douglas cocked the Sten, and doing his best to avoid standing on Feltham, poked his head cautiously out of the cab again. The explosion had reduced the rear end of it to a tangled wreck and he could see the marks left in the mud by its passage into the minefield. From somewhere, not far away, a bird was cheerfully trilling.

Six or eight Chinese soldiers were in the process of crossing the track. Douglas had a snapshot view of their stocky, uniformed figures before he opened fire. The sound of the short burst was deafening after the silence.

The soldiers fell on their faces and began firing back. Once again, Douglas was obliged to cower down into the cab as bullets pinged and ricocheted off metalwork.

'Now you've done it, corporal.' Feltham exclaimed. 'You've been and gone and upset 'em.' His heart was beginning to thump in his chest at the thought of his possible demise.

The firing stopped as quickly as it had begun, allowing the determinedly cheerful bird to recommence its warbling. Not for long, though, it was rudely interrupted again, this time by a high- pitched voice.

'British soldier! You have two minutes to surrender! We have a mortar zeroed in on you. I do not wish to kill you, but will do so if I must. The clock is ticking.'

Douglas looked down at Feltham's face; contorted with pain

and beaded with sweat. 'We'll have to give it up, Jim. Sorry, mate.'

'Never mind being sorry, just fucking well get me out of here before they start using their pop guns again!'

Douglas took a deep breath and poked his head and shoulders out of the door once again. 'All right, we're coming out! There's a wounded man here. Give us a bit of time.'

'No time! You come quick!'

Douglas reached down and lifted Feltham partially upright.

'They're as anxious about an air strike as we are, but for different reasons.'

He was obliged to climb completely out of the cab this time, before he could drag his friend into the paddy field. As he did so, the sharp pain in his chest made him gasp.

'I think I've broken some ribs, Jim.'

Supporting Feltham as best he could, he edged along the exposed underside of the Bedford. The heady aroma of petrol fumes filled the air. Feltham muttered,

'Have you got a match handy? There's no need to make them a present of all those stores.'

Thirty yards away, half a dozen soldiers were lined up on the road with burp guns and rifles trained on them. Douglas stopped, and with his free hand reached into a pocket.

The voice called out. 'British soldier, be warned!'

'Cigarette!' Douglas shouted back

He lit one and tossed the burning match into a little pool of petrol that was forming beside the remnants of the lorry's ruined canopy.

'Let's go, Jim!'

Gripping the cigarette between his teeth and keeping to the track left by the lorry, he rushed the complaining Feltham towards the road and the soldiers.

By the time their captors had searched them, relieving them of their watches and every other item in their pockets; a moat of fire had formed around the lorry and plumes of black smoke were rising into the air.

'That was very foolish to set the vehicle on fire,' the English-speaking soldier told them.

'Sorry about that,' Douglas replied. 'It was an accident.'

The ages of the Chinese troops ranged from sixteen to one who looked like a wizened pensioner. Although they were quite obviously exhausted, they handled themselves with confident professionalism. Douglas was wrestled to the ground, and with a knee in his back, had his wrists tied together. By twisting his head he could see that Feltham was receiving the same treatment. He protested loudly.

'Tying us up don't make sense! Is there an officer here?'

A soldier bent and put his face close enough to Douglas's for him to smell his malodorous breath. 'I am a captain of the victorious Volunteer Army of The People's Republic of China.'

The pressure from the knee in his back eased. 'Then, sir, you must realise that my friend has smashed his leg. He won't travel very fast, or very far, with his hands tied, and neither will I. If you leave me untied, I'll be able to help him along. That air attack you're expecting could be here any minute.'

The three-tonner's petrol tank suddenly exploded, causing everyone to crouch down as a plume of black smoke shot high into the air.

Spurred on by thoughts of American ground attack aircraft homing in on this smoke signal, the captain issued decisive orders. Douglas was released and Feltham was allowed to lean on him as they were hustled up the hillside.

'Take it easy, for God's sake,' Feltham pleaded.

Douglas developed a stunning headache. Every breath he took wheezed in his lungs. It was a noise that, incongruously, reminded him of the grating sound made by the opening of a certain garden gate in that other universe he had once lived in.

Near to the summit of the hill,they were obliged to scramble into a trench. Feltham cried out with pain as he fell heavily and lay on his side grasping a bloodied leg with both hands.

'I hope those fucking gods on Olympus are satisfied.'

Douglas had rarely heard Jim swear so much; it was an indication of severe suffering. 'Haven't you got any morphine, or something, that you can give him, sir?'

He felt his temper rising when this question was ignored by the officer. Something dark and uncontrollable began to stir within him.

The trench became a tunnel, into which the daylight only penetrated for a short distance. One of the soldiers produced a small, box-like torch, to light their way, but now that he was feeling relatively safe from an air attack, the captain called a halt.

'You may rest for a few moments.'

Douglas helped Feltham sit down. 'Are you O K., Jim?'

'No, I'm not bloody O K. I can feel blood running into my boot. If I pass out, tell 'em they can go on without me. I'll get the next bus.'

Their captors stood over them in the darkness, smoking Feltham's cigarettes and having a murmured conversation.

Douglas decided that paying a compliment to the captain would do no harm.

'Thank you for this chance to rest, sir. I must say that your English is excellent.'

'I worked for six years for Murchiesons in Hong Kong. I escaped from there when the Japanese invaded,' the officer said, with evident pride.

Any further talk was made impossible by the unmistakable sound of U.S. Air Force Sabre jets, screaming overhead.

'We go!'

As the noise diminished they were urged on. Feltham was on the brink of passing out; relying on Douglas to haul him along the tunnel.

'Don't pass out on me, Jim!'
'I won't if you won't.'
'That's a deal.'

The Sabres came back. The noise of their passing was deafening. Cannon fire and the crump of exploding rockets, as the area was chewed up, added to the cacophony.

The soldiers appeared to be growing impatient with their slow progress. Douglas was encouraged to move faster by digs in his back with the muzzles of their guns. This, combined with a particularly uneven section of the tunnel floor, caused him to stumble and fall, taking Feltham with him.

In the darkness, his free hand encountered the unmistakable shape of a British steel helmet. His fingers curled around its strap, gripping it tightly as he was hauled roughly to his feet.

The tunnel ended at last and they emerged into another open trench.

Douglas was still clutching the steel helmet, but before any of his captors could pay attention to that fact, they heard a burst of small arms fire from quite close by; rifles, burp guns and the 'crump' of grenades. A skirmish had broken out between two opposing patrols just a few hundred yards away.

The officer produced a pair of binoculars from his haversack and leant on top of the trench wall to survey the scene. He swept the horizon until something caught his attention that forced him to emit a grunt. He turned and barked out orders. Four of the six soldiers went scurrying along the trench, bent low and attending to their weapons.

'I am leaving these two men to guard you. They have orders to kill you if you attempt to escape,' the officer said, thrusting his sallow face belligerently at Feltham and Douglas as they sat in the dirt, grateful for any respite. Without further ado he hurried off to catch up with his men who were disappearing round a bend in the trench.

The two soldiers left behind looked weary and fed up, but they were alert enough as they sat a few feet away, with cigarettes dangling from their mouths..

'Hey, any chance of giving me one of my own fags back?' Feltham slurred, emitted a sigh, and passed out.

One of the guards came forward, examining Feltham with tired eyes.

The jets chose that moment to return. The second soldier

looked skywards as they screeched overhead, flying at zero feet.

Douglas felt a prickling sensation in the muscles of his arm as the adrenaline flowed. He tightened his grip on the helmet strap and struck savagely upwards, aiming its steel rim at the exposed throat of the soldier peering down at Feltham. Here were old sensations returning to haunt Douglas. Once again, he was involved in a slow-motion dance of death. He had time to do all that was required of him. There was plenty of time to slice the soldier's windpipe with the rim of the helmet. Time enough as well, to take hold of the man's burp gun, yelling defiance in tune with the jets as he did so. Time enough to hold down the trigger and kill the second man with one long burst of fire. Even as this one was falling, the life- blood of the first soldier was pumping from his slashed throat, spurting over Douglas's filthy uniform.

In the space of four heartbeats, one soldier was dead and the other was dying. Douglas closed that one's mouth with a bloody hand, in order to cut off the awful sound he was making.

Now he could hear the Sabres returning for their strafing run. He dropped the gun and seized hold of Feltham.

'Let's get back down the tunnel, eh, Jim? It's quieter in there.' The wounded man was in no condition to answer him.

As he laboriously half dragged, half carried Feltham back down the tunnel, one part of his mind was able to think about the events taking place out on the green slopes. A Yank or British patrol had encountered a Chinese or North Korean one. Now, with complete domination of the air in the hands of the allies, they were probably struggling to distance themselves from the enemy before the war-planes carried out their deadly work; work that involved turning human flesh into mincemeat with cannon shells or burning them to death with napalm. Either way, those aircraft created a hell on earth for foot soldiers.

He was obliged to rest for a few minutes in the dark of the

tunnel. Hauling Feltham along was not easy, but he wished he'd brought one of the dead soldier's weapons with him as well. Even now the enemy might be approaching in the sinister darkness from either end of the tunnel; driven underground by the air attack. In his usual manner, he cursed himself for a fool for not thinking to relieve one or both of the dead soldiers of their water bottles. He had never felt so thirsty, added to which, Jim Feltham was stirring and returning to full consciousness. He had nothing to give the man to ease his pain.

'What's happening? Are you there, Doug?'
'Yes, mate, I'm here. I sorted things out and we're heading back.'
'Heading back? What the hell happened?'
'I'll tell you later. Come on. Let's get going before our luck changes.'

They eventually emerged onto a sunlit hillside and flopped down on the grass. There was no sight or sound of the jets or any other activity. The birds were singing and a slight breeze rustled the vegetation. Douglas rubbed a filthy hand over his equally filthy face. Had he just had a nightmare? His head was swimming with fatigue. He didn't know whether the pain in his ribs had been there throughout the last fifteen minutes or had just returned with a vengeance.

Below them, on the other side of the track, lay the smouldering remains of the Bedford, now reduced to the bare and blackened bones of its parts, like the skeleton of a prehistoric monster. Feltham managed to raise a short laugh.
'Upon reflection, Doug, I think we made a mistake in setting fire to the lorry. You could have gone down there and got us both a drink of water.'

Douglas searched about and found a length of wood among the debris that littered the grass. It was the ideal shape and length for Feltham to use as a crutch. He removed his own bloodstained tunic and tearing his shirt into strips, he wound them tightly around his chest. It gained him some relief from the incessant throbbing.

After descending to the track, they were able to limp slowly along, chiding each other for their lack of progress and describing what they were going to do with a pint of beer at the first opportunity. Although they expected to run into the enemy again, or suffer sudden death from a hidden marksman, a temporary peace seemed to have settled over that section of the countryside.

'I reckon they've all been given the afternoon off,' Douglas said, wishing that, for the sake of his ribs, his friend wouldn't lean so heavily on him.

To protect his armpit, Feltham had wrapped his battledress jacket around one end of his improvised crutch. 'I don't think we'll be able to wear this gear on the next Church Parade, do you, Doug?'

By the time they were picked up by an American unit in the late afternoon, Douglas Bowen and Jim Feltham were two human scarecrows in a state of collapse.

'God bless America!' Feltham mumbled, just before he passed out in the back of the jeep.

12

End Game

It has occurred to me that you now know a whole lot more about me than I do about you. However, in the words of the late, great Jim Morrison, **'THIS IS THE END'**. Except, remember those asterisks you came across as you struggled to reach this point? Well, by some extraordinary coincidence, strung together in a certain sequence, the names in question express the wish that I –

'Shaw Hope Hall Theiss Wordsworth Evry Pound tu Spender!

George Bernard Shaw: Playwright and Critic 1856-1950

Anthony Hope: Novelist 1863-1933

James Norman Hall: Novelist 1887-1951

Ursula Thiess: Actress (Cor!) 1924-2010

William Wordsworth: Poet 1770-1850

Evry: Suburb of Paris

Ezra Pound: Poet and Critic 885-1972

'Tu'. A more intimate French form of address than 'You',

Stephen Spender: Poet and Essayist 1909-1995

'Suddenly it's Winter'

'As I left the green acres of the park
The road ahead seemed - just a little dark.
The year has passed so quick and swift away
Surely spring was only yesterday?
Exhilarated then by all those pristine days
I travelled many a highway and bye-way.
An early summer found me in the world,
Voyaging uncharted seas; all sails unfurled.
Kind fate brought me to an enchanted bay
Where I dropped anchor for a joyful stay.
Then, at the solstice, I chanced upon
An Eden isle, complete with Eve
There being no forbidden fruit
Or serpent, compelling us to leave,
We delved and spun, enjoined as one
Beneath a mellow autumn sun.
But suddenly it's winter and I am going home.
It's growing cold, with colder yet to come.'

'Bye, then.

Made in the USA
Columbia, SC
29 September 2017